Living with Awareness
Book 2

# Juggling the Pyramids

## Exercises, Games, and Rhythm Setting

Living with Awareness
Book 2

# Juggling the Pyramids

## Exercises, Games, and Rhythm Setting

by

Nalli

ISBN: 1-58820-991-1

Cover design is by Drake Brodahl.
Illustrations/graphics are by Diana Schuppel and Linda Olson.
The three roses are by Pat MacInnis. May you bud, blush, and
bloom daily.
Back cover photograph by Paul Nally.
Printed in the United States of America.
This book is a prescribed self-vaccine against self-psycho-blur.
Contact those responsible at:
**Mike Nally**, Ph.D.
623 Whispering Pines Lane, Suite 2
PO Box 611
Coeur d'Alene, Idaho 83816-0611
Telephone: 208.676.8126

This book is printed on acid free paper

1stBooks - rev. 11/27/00

# A Dedication
## In memory of my many friends and teachers.


I pause here to remember those whose paths have crossed and joined with mine, and who have added good fortune to my journey.

I nod in acknowledgment at the long blurred line of historic figures--of all cloth: playmates, extended family (an excellent blend of characters), school mates, special companions, friends, curious passers-by... especially the old elevator attendant at the Diamond Department Store in Charleston, West Virginia, in the late 1940s--a true "up-and-down" vertical philosopher.

Leaping decade to decade I come to memories of so many special people--the list is too long to itemize. With blessed affection I note: V, Pal, Gemma, Joan, Colleen, Don, Carissa, Pam, Tess, Jane, J.B., Granny, Jim, Dave, my granddaughter Laura, my grandson Michael, and my boyhood dog Ladybug.

**I thank you. I love you.**

# Milestones

# Writer's Comment

Q:  Why did I write this book?
A:  Because a funny thing happened to me on the way to the
    forum.  I discovered that there isn't one.., for me.

    I wonder what the thoughtful Roman did during the fall of
that empire.

    These pages contain suggestions and ideas of awareness
exercises, games, and rhythm setting that you may choose to use
to join in creating a forum for community and relationship; a
forum where we may meet in all aspects of self.  May harmony
and joy be your good fortune to share as you create a living path
with heart and dignity, using humor, respect, patience, and
productive activity as your guide posts.  May Awareness be with
you.  Awareness is not only how I define the Force, Awareness
<u>is</u> the Force.

# Exercises

## Thoughts and Ideas about Mood and Attitude. A party mix of pretzels, and nuts, and some crunchies, I hope, for everyone

"Life is like playing a violin solo in public and learning the instrument as one goes on." (Samuel Butler) The people who seem never to respond, or to adjust, or to improve their production of squeals and screeches in living are those who least practice awareness. To age without placing at least a brick or two in your Path of Wisdom, or without mastering at least three chords on a ukulele is a tragic waste of creative potential.

When you see someone who excels in a sport, or opera, or dance, or writing, or music, or relationship, or whatever area of living, you can be reasonably certain that they practice, exercise, and apply themselves daily in a full measure of concentrated effort at what they excel in. Aware practice may not make you perfect, but it will certainly make you better. A favorite saying (among many) of mine is: "The more I practice the luckier I get." Has there ever been a great golfer who said, in candor, "I depend on luck to win"?

When toiling in the field of creating a life, it works best for me when I avoid trying to be perfect or marvelous, and simply aim to be three steps past <u>good</u>. Good (social) is more likely to be within the range of my possibilities... and <u>good</u> is a pace that is "sweatable" for me on a moment-by-moment daily basis.

Is a yawn and a happy smile better than a migraine and a

1

barking grimace?  Just as you set your alarm clock at bedtime, set your daily attitude each morning at the first wake-up call. Decide then, and periodically throughout the day, that you will respect everyone you encounter... including yourself.  Open your "awareness option," increase your joy-level and harmony by creating respect, humor, patience, and productive activity in your daily affairs.  For you caffeine-and-sugar bunnies a nice add is medjool dates and double espresso.  Give the freeway "bump and grind" the gift of respect.  It will do wonders for your mood, for your blood pressure, and for your daily productivity.  Humor is the most patient of the senses.

Make yourself a "mirror sticker."  A private, in-your-bathroom awareness-sticker that can be moved on the mirror. Move it, and read it at each mirror visit.  Let vanity's motive work in your favor.  Those stick-on small note-pads work, but wilt with steam.  Here's a quote I spotted in a southwest Texas gas station's men's room:  "Do life... get outa Texas.  Despair sucks!"  You may prefer others--"Smiley faces" work for some people.  Personally, I do better with words.

Two sayings I use are:  "A monk's work is never done!" and the "Old Hickory" (Andrew Jackson) line, "Damn the man who knows how to spell a word just one way."  I display these two to myself in my briefcase, which I use as a daily companion and portable office.

Get rid of your plastic plodder's personality, if you want to be debt free in the world of relationship.  Don't be on a mission, be on a quest.  Be aware of your personal motives and purposes and how they might best support social attitudes in your daily affairs.  Instead of dropping numbly at day's end on the "burnout" pile in front of the TV, raise an energized chorus of amazed "Hello, what have we here" about the social value of aware choices and activities.  Be socially fit, not anti-socially flabby.

A primary awareness-perker for me is: Each day I write on my friendly Daily Reminder:  Patience--awareness--respect--humor--productive activity.  I reflect upon applying these guides to my list of tasks and I welcome them as distress-reducing agents when needed. I put these reflections, in various order, at the top of the page. At the bottom I write: "A dragon hoots!" Or I may use: deals, frets, craps, grins, barfs, etc. This is to remind me that "Camelot" has a dragon on the porch. There are serious problems in living that call to me daily in challenge. I do this exercise as an act of genuflecting to the day. Every time I check my calendar of events, which is frequently, and I see these word-tips my pace steadies, my mood whinnies, and my awareness soars... (well, almost soars).

A friend, Bob Venard, and I agree (as you also may) that it is useful to decide, event-to-event, during the day what mood/attitude you want to be armed with. Establish some mood-set moments: 1) When you wake-up, as mentioned, 2) when driving, 3) at work, 4) when relating and sharing with family, friends, or strangers, or 5) when alone, for example.

How do you want your living currents to flow: Calm or frantic? Pleasant or angry? Thoughtful or manic? Seek to be consistent and to have socially (the key word here) effective mood carry-over from one event to the next. For example, is it socially effective to have a calm attitude when scouring dried egg yolk from cold dishes... not being angry at the kids for not soaking their breakfast plates,.. but then screaming in explosive irritation at your spouse who makes a passing comment about the dirty car. Seek socially effective moods that are consistent and additive and you'll find your friends are many. I thank Bob for the example above.

Is it possible to have fun and to share creative episodes? Do you feel that your life is the butt of some space-age joke--that you're the punch-line of some cruel fate? How can you pop the blister of stress's rub? Do you believe in the practice effect? Or do you think that there's no room in living for practice?

It has been reported that National Geographic magazine photographers print only <u>one</u> picture of 466 taken--and these folks are considered to be pro's. The 465 "practice" rejects don't

3

seem to discourage them.  There's a moral here that can boost the morale of even the most <u>faux-pas</u> prone among us.

## Some ideas provided by friends, ex-spouses and frontier folklore

Each morning ask your roommate how to spell and define a word... and ask them (include your children) to do the same with you. Share your spellings, and definitions, then join in looking up the words in a dictionary. Use more than a pocket dictionary,.. perhaps an Oxford, or American or Webster's Deluxe. Look at the word roots and example uses. Remember this is an awareness exercise, it is not an exam. This can be a nice humor exchange, a learning and sharing moment for some people. See if it fits your taste, style, and interest.

Here's an idea that sounds like it could be a "schizotrek" (my coinage) warm-up. It's a point-of-view and change-of-pace fun exercise... so be sure to stay on this side of your reality line. The way this exercise goes is: Assume a different historical character's personality during social gatherings, or other opportunities of your choice. I would suggest you avoid the deep weirdo-types and pick the more thoughtful choices, such as Socrates, Chicken Little, Lincoln, Twiddle Dee, Stonewall Jackson, Big Bird, Mother Teresa, Elmer Fudd, Betsy Ross, Billy Graham, Tom Dooley, Abigail Adams, Al Einstein (ol' One Stone), Ms. Statue of Liberty, Ben Franklin, Lassie, or a curious, eager child you've known, perhaps.

If this list doesn't excite you, read-up on a character whom you admire. Then try viewing fun events and engaging lighthearted issues as you think that person would. This is a terrific way to open the pores of your awareness. But don't tie your own psyche knot too tightly, or hang-out in the twilight zone too long. Mensa midgets are so much spare change, on stress's subway to oblivion.

Some people use a daily <u>cue</u> word of common sightings to relax and focus their mood during the passage of the day. Colors are good cues. Others use the available cue situations and "clocks" in the environment. For example, a red stop light,

5

riding an escalator, when picking up a phone, taking a sip of coffee, using a rest-room air hand-dryer, looking in a mirror, or simply finishing reading or writing a letter. There are many cues,.. pick a few and use them to relax at each occasion. Relaxing and focusing are great awareness elevators--breathe in deeply, let your shoulders hunch toward your ears, and let that tension melt away as you exhale... also deeply... fully... and loooong. (Whoops, I almost nodded off.)

"To live well," it has been said, "hold forth enthusiasm at all times." I've found this to be a difficult task--but everybody knows that living, in any mode or gear, is tough. To accept and recognize the (so-called) bad times along with the (so-called) good times provides a balance and harmony in living. Without enthusiasm the balance of living slants toward boring and depressing. Awareness usually answers Enthusiasm's call.

Enthusiasm is attractive, fresh and exciting; it blows the staleness and dust from the flower of security with a whisper of risk and respect. It can also be quiet and personal, as enthusiasm in creative thinking is. Or it can be as actively humorous and visible as a free-running, tickling spring breeze in a silver maple tree. Enthusiasm as you create it in games, or dating, or other social interactions is the by-product of productive activity. And awareness is the cornerstone of all productive activity.

Knowing why and how to choose your companions, knowing how long to stay in a game, or when to hold a note in your daily aria are useful skills in effective living. Awareness is a critical addition to experience, if one seeks wisdom. Experience is a grand compass, but alone it is not, by a long shot, error-free or rust-proof. In fact, experience without awareness is a lousy teacher.

Carry yourself strong, not weak; light, not heavy; erect, not slumped. Posture, attitude (mood), and awareness have "much to do about everything." When you feel your confidence diving, check the elevation of your chin. Lift it! You could be amazed by the change in your appearance and your attitude by such a simple act.

What you do with your chin (Is he kidding?) has a direct influence upon your mood. A hanging, ducked chin bows your head, leads your eyes downward, slumps your shoulders, puts a shuffle in your pace. Shyness, uncertainty, and anxiety can blossom from such a habit. Not much room left for awareness, to be sure. An elevated, lifted chin brings the eyes and head along with it. Alert, assertive, energetic feelings grow in such posture. A chin held comfortably, firmly levels and brightens the eyes, puts confidence in your mood, lightens your step, braces the shoulders. Be aware of whence and where your chin roams.

When you feel fear stalking your mood, lift your chin! Life's challenges are easier to face when your chin is not on your shoe tops. Most challenges do not come from the tops of your shoes.

Good posture will keep you well in front of stress's posse. In facing daily challenges, forget the old warning in boxing: Do lead with your chin! For true grit, get your chin up. Be aware of how and where your chin is slumming. If you are blessed with several chin-chins, lift'em all.

For centuries soldiers the world over have been taught to TUCK, not DUCK, their chins. The idea is to square-up. This permits the natural poise, pride, rhythm, harmony, and grace to occur in movement and attitude. Who wants to see a bunch of GI's walking around with their heads hung down as if looking for their pacifiers?

As you may know, awareness enjoys the company of relaxation... and some people use sex as a major relaxer. Ahhh, I like skin on skin... but I prefer it not being my own on my own. Sexual pleasures in combination with a hot bath or shower are popular stress recesses. A friend told me of "wetting" his bed one night. He dreamt he was in a delightfully warm jacuzzi with Mary Magdalene. He claimed, despite the chore of clean-up, it was a highly redeeming experience. He is, by the way, no longer in the priesthood.

How about the use of soft colors to reduce stress and cue relaxation. Research wouldn't exaggerate, would it? Many people, especially pilot-types, seem to enjoy "wearing shades" to convert the world to bright green... others prefer light amber. Does this relax them, or just add to their "cool" image?

Here's a "mood breakfast" that may put some grits in your eggs. Each morning laugh yourself awake... but no hysteria, please. Fear and pain shrink away with a light dose of laughter. Start with a smile to get your mood moving upward... then welcome the new day with a laugh. It's double fun when you have a special friend to share the laugh. It's not quite as good by yourself,.. and it's a detour of deception when with a road-kill, one-night-stand left-over.

An old saying holds: "A smile is acceptance; a frown, rejection." Smile at each new day. Smile at each challenge.

A challenge is a great way to jump start your energy. Welcome each challenge as the companion it is. If the challenge is such a monster that all you can muster is a smirk,.. then smirk as hard as you dare. It might just slip into a smile.

What this living is all about is Situational Contextual Awareness Training,.. or SCAT! Rhythm and awareness exercises and stretches. Borrow ideas from friends, use some you find in these pages, make up your own--but do something. Living starts with doing, and creative living is a reflection of socially aware doing. I've never met a productively active person who was depressed.

Splash cold coffee (yesterday's) on your face as a wake-up gesture. A lady, a stranger I met on a bus ride from Sacramento to Modesto, told me about this ritual. She swore it was great for skin tone and color. I'd rather not judge, but, if it was working, I'd hate to see her without it. A major contributory effort in human progress, in her mind, would be a global industry for used coffee grounds. "An ignored recycle-able," she claimed. "A gold mine." To my regret she de-bussed in the Lodi area without disclosing the mine's exact location. However, she did suggest, in her "coffee-splash" advice, that I put my tongue firmly in my

8

cheek as I do it. Some interesting "bumps" exist on America's highways.

Practice concentrating. Concentration: that state of relaxed awareness so enabling in so many activities, interaction, and enterprises. Begin, as you would in conditioning your body for a sport, with short time spans of intensity. You might choose to watch the wind move a leaf, or a water drop run its crazy path down a window pane--then close your eyes and see the event again in your memory. Or read a few lines from a book, be a keen witness to a flying bird, a butterfly, a drifting cloud, embers faintly breathing at the touch of a soft evening breeze, or a twig coursing along on a laughing stream. Begin with brief episodes... being alert to moments and events which set up natural opportunities to practice your awareness skill-ability. Every scowling driver, every playing child can help you improve.

Come to know when you need a dose of quiet, alone time. Do not underestimate the restorative impact of solitude. Permit yourself to be as aware of this need for solitude (when stimuli overload your circuits), as you are aware of needing a drink of water. When you become so aware, have the good sense to provide it. Get yourself some space that is full of solitude.

While in graduate school in the late 1960's and early 1970's I worked in the area of developing (with Dick Suinn, Ph.D.) visual imagery as a stress management skill in athletes. This is now a popular, widely used practice in attempting to reduce pre-shot-game-event-bout jitters from tee-ball to teeing-off in the P.G.A. Many people would like to believe that visual imagery will enable you to perform beyond your ability. This is, of course, not what occurs. For miracles try frequent "tongue-in-cheek" coffee-splash facials.

Visual imagery is a practice exercise to heighten concentration (relaxed awareness) during challenge situations. Visual imagery does not "give you game that you ain't got." It does not dictate beyond-ability performance in some robotics, automatic fashion. Visual imagery, well-practiced, puts skill-

9

enabling concentration (relaxed awareness) available to the performer at the moment of challenge. Relaxed awareness and "out-of-body" experiences are located in vastly different parts of one's personal universe.

Police officers, soldiers, actors, students, teachers, athletes, doctors, nurses, parents, children, surgeons, writers (even me), lovers (even me, again), the relating public... the list seems endless... can gain in performance, in creating the life-moment of their choice, by strengthening their ability to concentrate. Use it in first meetings, first dates, the confessional... everywhere. Liberal doses of relaxed awareness are a dandy habit with which to stuff your pockets full.

# Let's call this section Kernel #2 1/2

Talk to at least one sane person each day, for no less time than it takes you to establish a firm contact with humor, patience, respect, and productive activity.

Spend a minimum of <u>15</u> minutes of each hour, <u>listening</u>... pure, aware listening. Listen to life. Listen to the context of the world around you. Concentrate on the act of listening. Listening is an art of great joy and comfort! Visually imagine that.

We talk, quite often, when we are anxious, ill-at-ease, pushy-nervous. To truly listen you have to have relaxed awareness (concentration), and patience, and respect. The wise person is an avid artist of listening. Reading is a form of listening--have you noticed? You must read, since you're here. Are you listening?

Listen with <u>all</u> your senses; listen with your eyes, nose, hands, skins, ears.... Listen to life in each created moment, each exchange; listen with all aspects of self. Be an artist of listening, be wise. Share the beauty of your skill and spirit. Listen attentively,.. even when alone. Be aware that you are listening. Tell yourself: "I'm listening."

Ante-up a smile when you join with another person, in company or in passing. Be more than a rider on the bus, more than a plodder in the parade, more than a spectator in your passage.

Do you ever join with and say goodbye to people listed in the daily newspapers' obituaries? Not a lot of us do. To read the brief summary of now "gone" people's journey is, for me, a glance through history (theirs) and a hint of the future (mine). I like to say to them, "It's over, (their first name), time to get off the pony." This helps me realize (be aware) that living, which ends every second for someone, is all too quickly and eternally gone. In debate, some people argue that--not to worry--we

11

return in other life forms or bodies. About such things I am not, yet, privy, nor concerned.

To pout over spilled cold porridge or swat at imaginary gnats are poor time investments when time is so limited. When looking over an obit, especially when my therapist has called in sick, I feel a calm, attached interest... in letting reality blur. The fallen soul resting now by the roadside of generations brings me to Heidegger's awareness crossroads: the possibility of <u>not being</u> intersects my appreciation that I <u>am</u>.

I enjoy, as a daily reminder, to recall: "Good fortune is a responsibility to be <u>shared</u>." To be <u>shared</u>. Ah, good fortune is a very human state--a state which includes <u>others</u> and aware interchanges.

Meditating is self-listening. To meditate/listen periodically throughout the course of each day is to set a pace which permits humor, respect, patience, and productive activity to flourish along the path of your awareness from early 'til late, short and tall, wide and narrow, far and near.

Recall often those loved ones who live beyond the fences and fields of your daily visits. I use the early morning routine of rinsing my face awake to say greetings to my daughters and grandchildren--Hello, Carissa! Hello, Pam! Hello, Tess! Hello, Laura! Hello, Michael! One rinse, two rinse, three rinse, four....

Whenever I find a coin on the ground, in my many strolls and wanderings, I say hello to a dead relative or friend. I like to stay in touch--some days I say hello a lot. A penny will make a call all the way to heaven (or to hell). Hi, Mom! Hi, Dad! Hi, Gemma! Hey, gang! If finding coins isn't your thing, you could perhaps say "Hey!" when you spot a lonely wild flower beboppin' in the wind, or an out-of-state car plate, or when you hear a crow cawing, or when an owl calls your name. Staying in touch is important. I also use found golf balls, nails and such, and aluminum cans as special tokens to pause in memory. There's some family history involved, for me, with these items. There exists a forest full of memory cues--choose a few of your liking and mark the pages of your memory with them.

To fret at boredom's chains of distraction try using words in fresh ways. Somebody has to invent new slang and metaphor... why not you? If you need a steady supply of ammunition, cruise a "good" dictionary, often. Much of our history is found in our words; our words can be found in the tombs we call dictionaries.

Dictionaries are full of secrets, silliness, shadows, superbness, and the down-right strange. These books <u>are</u> the trail of human thought and invention. The other day I was checking the spelling of "psychomimetic." A word I hadn't used or heard since graduate school days--and I have no plans to ever use it again. It wasn't to be found in my Deluxe Webster's, and may, in fact, be misspelled here. If my dictionary is a witness, the word may be mere condensation from the heat-oppressed mind of a weary, but highly motivated, graduate student. It may not have a history. As I searched the pages sorting the <u>Kraut</u> from the <u>UnKraut</u> I discovered the word: "psychopannychism" (the belief that the soul falls asleep at death and does not awake until the resurrection of the body). A word obviously rooted in a religious belief, foreign and novel to me. A maze of surprises my dictionary, a garden of <u>Kraut und UnKraut</u>.

This psychopanny word, except as the pollen of past human invention, is useless to me. But because of its value to others, past and, perhaps, present and future, I give it a <u>6</u> on the Interesting Scale. Ah, the awareness, the secrets that wait for us. Gems to be discovered and then polished as we fondle them in our minds.

As Thomas Gray told us, "Full many a gem of purest ray serene, the dark unfathomed caves of oceans bear...." With a dictionary you don't need SCUBA gear to dive into the depths and folds and tunnels of the caves of human invention. Follow the words.

Every time you look into a mirror, or see your reflection in a window, give yourself a boost. Lift your chin, smile and tell yourself, "Think funny! Think creative! Don't stagnate!" Be sure to stir in a "silly" look. Silly looks help me separate the smoke and the flames in this stressed, skid-marked world.

13

Get loose and relax. "Think crazy!" It feels surprisingly nice... and is marvelous for the <u>Gesundheit</u>. Such attitude cues are especially useful on the "8th day of the week." When that nagging telephone sends an irritating bean up your nose, or wherever. Give yourself an attitude lift. The person on the other end of the line doesn't deserve vinegar and urine, and neither does your business reputation, nor do you. Work on your social flexibility and self-awareness. Answer the phone, perhaps, in a different character-pitch (Forrest Gump was popular in the spring of '95). Pick your voice within our vast pantheon of characters from entertainment, fame, or politics. Such imitation has done wonders for the enduring renown of Bugs, Gabby, John Wayne and the Roadrunner. Telephone answering machines have brought the best (in some) and the worst (in some) center stage. "Ham" is back on America's menu.

A yawn is a quiet way to shift gears. Some people pride themselves in being able to orally or anally pass gas on command, while others prefer to master the yawn. The yawn creates, when witnessed by others, an imitative response of relaxed slow-down. That same collective feeling from a burp or a fart has yet to come to my notice. When the incursion of rudeness is excused as humorous inquiry and creativity I fail to discern the poetry from the prose, the flower from the thorn, the Q from the A. With a yawn as my escort I bow to my awareness and I get the Winken, Blinken, and Nod out of there.

## Kernel #3  Sorting is one thing, perfect sorting is quite another... and it's definitely not my thing.

A few suggestions for keeping your day snag free.

1)  Don't open any mail from an attorney-at-law.  This is a sworn to "no-no" by a dear friend.  He says that lawyers never write fun letters.  If they could, they wouldn't be lawyers, he is convinced.
2)  Ignore all phone calls not screened through an answering machine.
3)  Don't spend time with demanding, spoiled children, even when they're your own.
4)  Avoid conversations with spouse, boss, IRS agent, or police that start with, "You're not going to like this, but...."
5)  Stay at least 1 1/2 time zones from all "rush hour" (now there's a strange use of words) traffic.
6)  Beware of "drinking holes" named "ONE MORE FOR THE ROAD," and of girls named "Bambi" (wasn't Bambi a male?).
7)  If you're walking through a part of town that requires you to carry a gun,.. you're in the wrong place and carrying the wrong resume.  At times like this... speed is your friend.
8)  And remember:  "Don't play cards with a guy named Doc;.. Don't eat at a place called Mom's;.. Don't go to bed with anybody who has more troubles than you do." (Nelson Algren)

If you have suggestions for this list, please, let me know. Avoiding car salesmen named "Honest Harry" comes to mind... as I write.  If you can completely avoid the items listed, I think you don't live in the U.S.A.

I'll close this part by thanking my friend Jim (the Shoe) for his many suggestions (I trashed them all) and by saying to you: Have a snag free one! ... you too, Jim. Isn't it interesting, even scary, how we psychologists pretend to know people so well... and not? Many of us have book-smarts, but scant street and daily-activity smarts. We claim to know others, but have no working relationship with self. In my muddled understanding of living I often remind myself of the startled mugger who said to the gone-ballistic shopped-weary muggee, "Hey, whoa! Let me clarify our roles here."

## This section I'll call "Hi, Terri!" Terri is typing this thing... from my hand-written (aka scribble), on-yellow-pads mess. Thanks, Terri!

Pump up those bike tires, or air shoes, and go for a daily outing. I prefer a shaded path along a winding river, canal, or lake,.. or a wooded country lane. I try to avoid traffic, pollution, and pain-filled "head plants." I'm out cruising to relax, not to make war. I've come to grips, more than once, with the flip-side of my sanity during a casual walk with a friend.

Invite Uncle Wiggly and Uncle Remus to join you on your walks. They know every tune ever hummed, and they bring joy to any party. Plus Mother Nature holds them in special affection. She often graces their day with sunshine.

While walking, if only across a room, listen to the tone and melody of your body and mood. Don't let "Jaded" become your name, or your game. Let your attitude hitch-a-ride on some models. For example, I always admired my Granpa Palkovic for his marvelous positive physical posture and carriage, and for his inspiring interest in staying involved in full-purpose living. He worked as a professional horticulturist until he was 96 years old. A current hero of mine is my 90 year old golfing buddy Ivan. Ivan stays fully-engaged in restoring and selling houses, travelling to visit his many friends of all ages, and volunteering

17

to help the elderly. Ivan, until recently, walked our hilly golf course, and his golf-goal is to shoot his age. Such people should live a thousand years, at least.

Should your shoe come untied while you are on a walk (not a run or jog... too trippy) don't tie it. Let it flop. Take a break from routine, and habit, and compulsive form. A loosely laced, tightly knotted shoe is less likely to demand attention, than is a tightly laced, loosely or tightly knotted one. I enjoy all this detail-awareness stuff. Compulsiveness and loosely laced, double-knotted shoes are what got some of us through graduate school.

Your daily walk is a special chance for rippling through the file pages of your past. Pick a time at random and let the pages loosely flip. It's impressive how the mind and memory work. This exercise--no matter the time, age, or events that pass in review--is one of amazing grace and awareness. After all, it is the past, your past. These pages of your foundation tell you where you have been, they do not dictate where you may go. Scan them comfortably, for they are as safe as you permit them to be. Make your past work for you, not against you. Let it be your fuel, not your burden.

Do you remember the song: "Count your blessings... la, la, la... and you'll la, la, la, counting your blessings"? Some folks believe this "counting your blessings" is a dandy way to harvest optimism. A friend said, "I feel blessed every time I zip-up my 'fly' and don't feel tender skin in metal teeth." He is one of those ready recruits into the school of "blessings counters," but one who relies a great deal upon realism.

Every moment of every day begins with your choice regarding your social responsibility and direction. "To be, or not to be," someone once wrote, "that is the Q." (His initials are W.S.) To be, or not to be, what? Is my Q. To be socially responsible, or not to be socially responsible--is a good choice. People who choose **to be** mature, who choose to create relationship with others and Nature, who choose **to be** aware, who choose to create a harmonious path of respect, humor,

18

patience, and productive activity, who choose to create social balance and rhythm, they are the spiritually wise who choose **to be**... joy-filled.

We are surrounded by awareness cues and automatic clocks in our "debt-shackled" system. How about these "star-speckled" flags: Standing in line, traffic slow-downs, people-gluts, and T.V. commercials? What marvelous occasions in which to relax. Don't let stress set the pace. Every crowd-encounter, traffic-wad, toilet-clog, electronic-glitch, or sales-drone is a chance to create a relaxation-awareness moment. Any "Big Bens" working in your world? If you have any favorite relaxation clocks, drop me a note, I'm interested.

I've found juggling to be a relaxation-concentration exercise of daily choice for me. I'm not ready to go on tour, but I can move a few objects in the air. Juggling is an ambidextrous (two handed) challenge--it's fun, and it enlivens a person. If you're a type "A", "110%" kind of personality who hates to give up distress, start with five or six tennis balls and work your way down, from total frustration, to a level of "maybe I can do this." If you get down below one ball, I'm not sure what that's called. But if it relaxes you, keep doing it.

This "Gaukler" is no stress glutton--I choose relaxed awareness in my daily passage. I juggle only in short spurts. I keep a few small beanbags available, for when I get a craving. Juggling provides ample bend-and-reach exercise, as well, until you learn how to catch the darned things. Gravity does work. I find bean bags to be a bit more retrieval-friendly: less bounce and roll than tennis balls. If you decide to try bean bags, I recommend that you cut, stuff, and sew them yourself. Challenges come in many shapes and sizes.

There are many ways to put some "fruit loops" in your living diet--as many ways as there are imaginations to create them. "It won't get better," the saying holds, "until you let it." Want a new point of view? Put your imagination on "play".... Spin your head and your heart on finger tips, toss them into the air,.. better

19

close your eyes, you could get dizzy. Have fun getting rid of the humbug in your mood. Your imagination is a private playground, a special place where you can find "fruit loops" growing on every tree and bush--if you so choose.

A nice stress reducer and productivity increaser for the work place is time-pacing. Break your work into packets--set a timer if necessary--of 45 minutes of concerted, focused effort, then take 10 minutes for light exercise, stretching, a relaxation nap, a walk down the hallway... or whatever activity you prefer (no streaking, please--too disruptive). Many people find that with time-pacing their craving for cigarettes or coffee is less nagging.

The latest research in body rhythms and other such foxtrots suggests that every 90 minutes we need 20 minutes rest. Some employees, however, seem to have that turned inside out and backwards. Drop by a government agency office with a stop-watch and check it out. Some people work too hard, some hardly work at all. Burn-out and boredom are both dangerous viruses in the work place.

Work, then restore yourself, work, then restore,.. throughout the day. Your thoughts will gel during breaks, especially if you can avoid the smokes and caffeine jolts, and this will help your work quality, out-put level, attitude, energy, and safety. Stressed office workers are the ones with staples in their fingers and thumbs. "How about 5 minutes of work and 25 minutes of play?" Did you ask? Some are already on that pace. We call them salaried, tenured, no-case-load, terminal bureaucrats. Happy pacing!

Stroll along your mind's balance beam. Create shot-gun time travel in your imagination. Hopscotch the Horoscopes--read a line from any three (or more). I come up with some great reads. Kick a stone along a dirt road, or walk the roadside curbs while pretending to be a tightrope walker in the circus--but don't try this if your balance is shot-to-hell-terrible and you trip over carpets. I used to walk train rails for miles--with rarely a mis-step... but I gave up the rails,.. I'm not a kid anymore. I'm interested in awareness, not in injury.

Pirouetting, moon-walking, and break-dancing are enjoyed by some, neglected by others. I'm in the "others" group here. These were never some of my favorite things--a generational choice, no doubt. There are many things to do which get the blood pumping and the mood elevating.

Disco dancing was and still is popular--but, once again, not a first choice with me. Going to a dance to be separated, often lost, from your partner, doing five minutes of alone aerobics, or anaerobics, depending upon your style, in a crowd, to return to your table (if lucky, your partner will also return) to talk of what fun it was to be apart. This distance-dancing seems an odd choice of how to be together to a slow-dancing, up-close person like I am.

When a person says that Nat "King" Cole, Mel Torme, The Platters, and Tony Bennett are his/her singers of choice, you're not talking to a "buck and wing" kind of person. "Jitter bugging" is about as far as I like to be removed from my partner on a dance floor. Some of the Western Line Dancing is fun... but the part I like best is the adapted jitterbug turn-and-spin stuff!

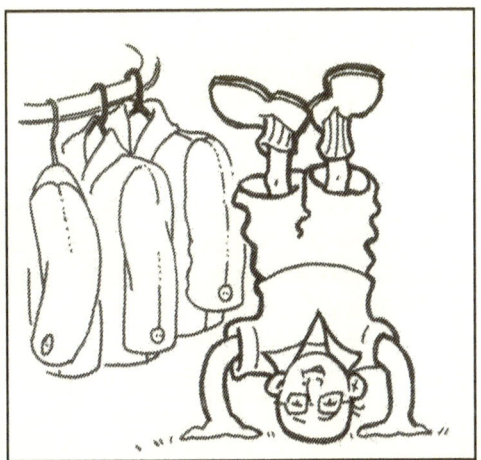

Do you ever stand on your head? I do. And unlike dancing I prefer to do it alone. Not too many people do couples or group head-standing, I think. A great place to do this when in a mall is among the racks in the clothing stores. They usually have "cushy" carpets, which are easy on the top of the head, or the butt should a tumble occur. Head stands are terrific for moving some corpuscles, but there is no proof they cause head hair to grow. More of us old

21

guys would be so inclined, permanently vertically inverted, if true.

Talk about blood pumping and mood elevating: Shopping as done today by many women has been called the most popular participation contact-sport in America. But, I join most guys here: shopping is not my sport of choice, no matter under what rules, or in what arena. This is another "go together, to be apart" activity for me. I simply cannot discover the thrill in shopping.

When I've agreed to escort a lady friend on a shopping safari, no matter how many shirts I touch or shoes I look at I end up boring-out, nodding-off, and looking for a secluded head-standing spot.

For me, head-standing (I go back, way back, in the racks far from the "madding crowds") not only moves the blood from my feet to my head, it is also a way to inventory my pants pockets. Let me suggest, for those females thinking of trying this event of public head-standing, wear trousers (long preferred). If not, you may find that you are not so alone as you might have hoped to be.... Follow?

I'm not sure that it's just my head-standing behavior, but I get few second-date requests to the mall. My chafed attitude-- diagnosed as "aisle" stress and "try-on" rash--may be a factor, as well. Actually, for me, <u>not</u> going to the mall is a great relaxer. Heck, I can head-stand in my living room, or in the park (watching-out for doggie "biscuits," of course).

A hint and a caution about curb walking. First the caution: You can break an ankle or worse, if your focus is willy-nilly. Do not drink and walk curbs. In a CWD (curb walking drunk) accident the leg you break <u>will</u> be your own. As in sky-diving, should you "plant" or otherwise injure a body, it <u>will</u> be your own.

Now comes the curb-walking hint: I do better when I get up on the balls of my feet and put some lift into my step. Perhaps, the heel to toe, heel to toe movement scares me just enough to turn up my concentration. Most activities, I can't think of any--

even sleep--that are excluded, go better when awareness, focus, and energy blend and flow in time, degree, and harmony. Even sex gains when productively active, rather than habitually appetitive.

Aerobics for peaking and toning the aspects of self: Hmmm, what comes to mind? Hiking (being in Nature's embrace), writing, reading, listening, feeling, sensing,.. being social... and how about going to church as a spiritual toning aerobic? Could it be? Or perhaps an art museum. Or a music festival. Or doing humorous art/music.

To rout distress some people hum, some whistle, some sing, some pray, and some use a "cheat sheet." To career couch-yams: watching TV is their idea of high impact involvement; putting on a shirt, their idea of an aerobic exercise; getting through Saturday morning cartoons, their idea of a mental challenge. On the bus-of-living, where everyone has to bring their own lunch and take their turn riding in the back, the couch jockey's idea of "religion" is praying that the tube doesn't blow.

Despite the appearance of comfort that money from a "good-living" supports, living-well is not without gristle and splinter. Living-well requires effort based upon concentrated social and ecological purpose. A hot dog is still a hot dog, no matter what type of mustard you use. When the "breaks" seem to be negative, do something positive for others and Nature. To delight in the success of others and in the glory of Nature will jump-start your awareness to the purr-level every time.

When you go out for fun, such as golfing leave the sour apple side of your personality buried in a cemetery for the day... you can exhume it later, if you must. Being all ass, twenty-four hours a day is hard on you and hard on others. To have fun on the golf course, share it with others. Don't hit into the group ahead, yell at a slow player, or throw clubs, balls, shoes, or rages. There are closets a-plenty for such tantrums.

Set yourself up to succeed: pick your spots and hit your shots. Should you decide to try juggling, don't try on the inside of a closed garbage bag--too snug, too dark. If you play golf for

23

social fun and companionship, don't let your soiled shorts and bad temper be all you have to contribute to the group.

Did you ever try "walk-by" isometric or isotonic exercising? "Walk-by" exercising is like grazing food in nibble-snacks rather than in large meals. A little done often throughout the day, rather than intense burn-sessions. Put a dumbbell with a less than hernia load in your bedroom or work site. When you walk by do a few reps. The livingroom floor invites stretches, push-ups, crunchies, head-stands. Your office chair and car are thrones for isometric exercising. Tone and strengthen is the goal, not strain and pain. When you know the plan is for a few, often... there's no pressure to do the 110% "'Roid Rage" routine. Your life doesn't have to be put on a hook, when your exercise focus is the pursuit of awareness, wellness, and fun-fitness. The jury is <u>in</u> on 110% stress-aerobics--Verdict: Return to sender! Put your awareness-wellness on a life-time fitness pace of balance and harmony.

This same "walk-by" method works for writing letters or books, visiting with colleagues and friends, thinking and creating, remembering and affection, recognition and acceptance, relating and sharing, humor and productive activity. Cram for an exam? No, thanks. I like to learn, not burn.

The good life, the path with heart and dignity, is created in a "walk-by" of balance and harmony. Stress is a "have-to" event, joy is a "walk-by" event. Joy has no melt-down moments, no burn-out blisters. Am I imagining things, or has Caffeine taken control of the building?

To check your personal awareness practice smiling or, if a frowner, practice un-frowning both when with others and when alone. Most of us don't smile much when we're alone. During the day are you exchanging smiles, or what, with the other dancers? Look at your reflection in available mirrors and store-front windows. Catch yourself smiling, if you can. How's the posture? What pocket have you got your chin in? How do you feel in all aspects of self. As sportswriter Jim Murray wrote of baseball great Roberto Clemente: "He's happy inside but his face doesn't know it."

Take a moment to enjoy the wind and rain in your hair. Listen! Is that rain on the roof? Relax and rest your attitude as the falling rain calls you awake... sounds like the happy little feet of 114 dancing squirrels,.. as refreshing as that smile you're about to practice.

Could it be that we don't enjoy the night's gift of darkness enough for our own good in this age of bright lights and distractions? Who do you know that sits quietly or strolls leisurely in the cool darkness shedding the stress and heat of the day? Who, in the general population, look in pleasure and poetry at the distant stars on a nightly break of restoration? Is sleep your only time-out for your in-high-gear senses? Let patience bloom! Patience will pack up all your care and woe,.. if you'll just give it a chance. The darkness oozes patience. Patience replaces scattered, frayed alertness with ordered, calm awareness.

Did you see the movie "Harvey" (title?) with Jimmy Stewart? It's about a man with an imaginary friend/companion named Harvey. To many who have seen it, it is a classic. Some people even remember the man's name. I'm not one of those, or I would have used it. People understand having an imaginary friend. Before this Age of Mass Distraction (a major industry planet-wide) every kid and many adults could be seen talking with non-existent people or animals (often dead parents or pets) as they played or strolled. Today we are busy inventing multiple personalities rather than imaginary friends... and loneliness is eating many of us from the inside out.

My opinion about having imaginary friends is: Without awareness and control of the reality parameters of the activity, it is probably diagnostically "crazy" to have dis-embodied companions. However, for the person who creates a living path; with awareness and healthy reality-contact not to have a wee elf or two is to deny Imagination its chance to dance. Do I have an imaginary friend? You bet I do... try several.

I take my Grandpa Palkovic (my mother's dad)--I call him Pa Pa Pal--on my daily walks. He is an excellent walker, has the best posture I've ever seen, a creative humor and a quick wit, enjoys Nature in all her seasons (he was a horticulturist, a gardener and grounds-keeper during his long life. He lived, in good health, well into his 90's), and nurtures an interest in many topics and events. Plus, he is unbelievable at finding golf balls, aluminum cans, and wayward coins.

Do I talk with him? What a question. I should ask him to join me, then not talk with him? I should be so rude? Being a born-again golfer I find the balls, the cans (recycled at market rate), and the coins useful. Next week I'm asking him to look for unbroken tees, I could use a few. If you have an imaginary companion, say "Hey!" from Mike and Pa Pa Pal. Uncle Remus and Uncle Wiggly often meet me down by the creek... and the crew of us zip-a-dee-doo-dah along.

Relax when you drive. Why not? Here you have a perfect set-up for relaxing,.. yet, you often ignore it. You sit in a comfortable, adjustable seat, heater and air conditioner (both often available), and a CV (Closevision as opposed to TV or television). A wide, wrap-around screen with an ever-changing picture for your viewing pleasure. Hey, an automatic remote control--how good can it be? Enjoy it. Relax while driving, cut your tense "rage" time by "bellows" each day.

Let eating be a cue, a signal, for relaxing. What a treat to relax in the awareness of taste, texture, and comfort of food. Even "fast food" could be a message rather than a mugging: try chewing as a pacer. "Fast food" does not mean swallowing whole bites.

How many of us use our trips to the toilet as private moments of personal relaxation? Only I know the answer as it includes me, and only you know your own. Aristotle would be disappointed that many of us regard his words about "life's greatest pleasure" so lightly in our serious dash of unawareness.

## Awareness toners.  Mental aerobics.

Break up your hand and eye habits.  Change the pattern of your daily rituals and behaviors.  Here are some "such as-<u>es</u>:"

Eat using your off hand once a week.  I recommend using a spoon.
Write with your off hand, now and then.
Wink with your off eye.  This is called turning a wink into a grimace.
Read with one eye; alternating each sentence.  Do you know which eye is dominant?
Clip your finger/toe nails in a different series.  Do you know your blood type?
Brush your teeth with your off hand, following a different route.
Brush your hair with the same off hand.  Take a risk.  Change your hair style... or, at least, how you part it.
Button your shirt/blouse one-handed and also vice versa.

Turn up the volume of your awareness.  Toss yourself a "cross-seams" fast ball, or an "off-speed" change-up, now and then, to perk your tempo and get you up on your toes.
For example, how about those toilet habits?  Do we dare alter hands here?  Can you--are you ready to be a switch wiper?  A serious attention grab, a major change of pace.  A potential "yuck!"
Shaving one's face... ah, now here's a ritual (usually a.m. type) that is absolutely made for awareness variation.  Face shaving is typically a guy thing (but not always) and as I do it, it requires a razor, a mirror, hot water, and shaving cream.  For a simple event it's a fairly high-equipment operation, actually.  It can be done with either hand... or for the highly dexterous with the feet... my throat tells me, "No way!"

27

The idea for using shaving as an awareness wake-up came years ago when an old-line Army Sergeant told me, "For a real loud wake-up call lick jelly off a razor's edge--with or without a hangover. Trust me, you'll pay attention."

I'm endlessly amazed at how many different ways there are to shave a face. It beats boring, and with a little caffeine it might help flip your headlights to high beam. Just the various ways to paint one's face with shaving cream are artistically endless. But you might not want to try this cream-bit, if you use an electric razor. A bit gummy for the ports, I think.

Another daily routine act for many of us (less so for "sweat hogs," "rednecks," and hermits) is toweling off after a bath or shower. Ever thought about alternating patterns here? Some people use two towels--one for the lower cheeks and pits, one for the upper cheeks and pits. Others like to put a Rumba into the rub. Adjust your routines, put some flowing circles in your stroke. This can be done with various body-parts in various situations of private or public (forget pubic here) drying opportunities.

Move your thoughts and body parts, within reason and social dignity, in slow circular and semi-circular motions; e.g., when toweling, or when using a hand-dryer in a public restroom (I've never seen one in a private home), or when strolling in a park (let your thoughts make "lazy circles in the sky"), or when playing golf (a highly semi-circular game), or when weaving a cat's cradle, or when attending your weekly Tai Chi class. And then, too, isn't breathing all about circular flow and motion? Who notices? I hope you do. Rotate your mind, mood, and body slowly, seeking to make all living motion a universal harmony and flow. Hmmm, it feels nice. Ah, let's take a moment,.. an aware life-time... to notice.

Revisit briefly past moments in your life. Stay with one age at a time. An excellent mental exercise to stir your psychic energy on those blah, low-pressure, cabin-fever days. Say to yourself, "I'm (you pick the age) years old and--." Let the

28

circles flow, let the notice grow, let the Past bring to the Present and the Future an aware, harmonious glow.

---

Just now, I have received word that a long-time friend Pete James is dead. A stroke suddenly took dear Pete out of the game.... And such a wonderful player he was. I am numbed by the toll of the bell.

Pete James, the man I knew to be of keen wit, humorous view, memorable laugh, and gentle spirit, is no more,.. forever. Excuse me. I'm going for a walk.

Come on, Pete, let's visit. Uncle Remus! Uncle Wiggly! Wait up, please. There is someone here I want you to meet.

---

I'm back. Much wiser, I hope. It was a two-walks day. Let's continue. Say to yourself, "I'm X years old and I'm ready to explore life!" When done with bright eyes, youthful conviction, and keen alertness such mind-travel can be polliwog heaven. Of course, if you never were 12 years old (the age I just picked), nor ready to explore the caves of your creative imagination, you won't have the foggiest notion about what I'm talking, or why I'm suggesting such off-ramps from our adulthood daily haste.

*Nalli*

## Memory stretches.

1) Do nothing! Can you? No feelings, sensations, thoughts--pure nothingness. The old saying: "Out of nothing, comes nothing" may be in for a stiff test here.
2) Recall foreign language words and phrases. Invent dialogues in foreign settings to Jibber-Jabber rap.
3) Close your eyes and let the kite of your imagination soar. Imagine being someone else, somewhere else. Create the person--don't use a known model--using a collage of admired values and character traits.
4) Focus on the aspects of self as they occur in you. How many aspects are you able to spend time with, how many avoid your invitation? How big is your personal temple; how grand, your images?

In your daily ramblings invent metaphors, similes, and analogies cross-linking the emotional, mental, spiritual and physical experiences of self to the social and natural exchanges, events and challenges of daily living. A card shark always has a deck of cards at hand; a word lover needs a dictionary in his/her lunch pail.

Hobbies to the left of us, hobbies to the right of us, hobbies of every imaginable sort have been human mood-massagers since our dawning. Let Awareness become a hobby, a living gift.

The hobby garden includes every manner of bloom--from collecting to building, from shopping to puttering, from crossword puzzles to jigsaw puzzles, from flowers to old cars. Stroll these fragrant paths and see if you find an interest. My interest/hobby is words, languages, cultures and writing (letters mostly,.. or a book, now and then). Learn of self by watching what you do, when you don't really have to be doing anything.

Which of these would you choose? Build a room on the back, bake a cake (from scratch), go to a staff meeting, bird watch, fish, golf, read, sex-up with someone, climb the highest mountain, collect stuff, exercise self aspects, or the popular etc.? Who <u>are</u> you? Do you run on AC or DC? How much time each day do you spend looking for your glasses? <u>How</u> are you <u>really</u> doing? <u>What</u> are you <u>really</u> doing? How broad is your valley; how high, your mountain?

There are physical (hup, two, three, four) exercises; mental (spelling, reading, writing, 4 x 8 = 32, 6 x 9 = 54) exercises; emotional (screaming, cooing, singing: "Smile tho' your heart is aching....") exercises; and spiritual (the creative arts are an expression of spiritual flexing, such as finger painting, or playing musical scales, or poetic musing--along a continuum of skills and moods) exercises. Are there any social and natural expression exercises of living and being? What comes to mind? Perhaps we can meet under an orange-colored sky, create opportunity and values as the wind and rain play in our hair, and "think tank" a few.

Voltaire, the well-regarded French philosopher, 1694-1778, (I looked this date up in my Webster's Deluxe Dictionary) told us: "Till your garden. It's the best of all possible worlds." Voltaire expressed this in French, I believe; and I also believe, among other paths, he meant precisely that--pull weeds (do not smoke them), pamper your lawn, vegetable-plot, yard flowers and shrubs, and house plants. Some people really know weeds, aphids, and winter kill. They seem to richly enjoy the leisure hours they spend toiling in meeting the assault of the invaders into their tiny garden kingdom--invaders on-loan from Mother Nature. To garden is to touch the magical germ of life as a special agent of God. A gardener can bring visible life to places it didn't exit before. My bro' Don, aka Weedman, is just such a happy pixie planter-and-puller. The Weedman speaks "plant language" very well.

A special evening of social nourishment and joy occurs when you cook for friends. Or even better, some people feel, is to get a friend to cook for you.  Food is a marvelous substitute for hunger; friends, for loneliness.  Share some veggies you've planted and pampered to life.  Let the poetry of your spirit bloom abundantly.  Listen to an infant coo, and you will hear the voice of Hope.  Devote less time to property and possessions and more time to people and plants.

Send Mother Nature a fax that carries your boots and your butt deep into her charming, interesting, challenging and mysterious office.  Camp, hike, sail, bike,... get grungy, kickback, relax.  Fortunately, a friend of mine owns a small cabin in the San Juan Islands off the coast of Washington.  Each year a group of fellows--of diverse ages, interests, backgrounds, career fields, experiences, and tolerances for close living and snoring--gather for our "male bonding and spitting" time.  We have had to limit our number to twelve, lest we find ourselves in a small town of lines and gridlock.  The fact that all of us go to a fair degree of trouble each year to be in attendance, says this social visiting of friends in the restoring protection of Nature holds something of special value for each of us.  (I'll visit you, Pete. Thanks!  Pete, a twelve year veteran, now comes only in spirit.)

"Women give birth to children; men give birth to machines and motors."  This is a line I heard as a boy.  As I now turn it in my mind, I have to admit that my over 60 years "of watching people" support the idea.  Women seem to like children because it lets them mother, men seem to like machines and motors because it lets them control.

The rest of my boyhood line says, "and both have dogs as their best friend."  No matter how you shake or stir it, babies, machines, motors, and pets all can be incentives to aware involvement.  I personally prefer people and animals to motors and machines.  How do you feel about re-arranging furniture?

"Cut the crap!" exercise.  Play no "head" games with self or others.  The only winners in "head" games are the toilets.  Are you a toilet?  Be aware of your games--cut the crap!  When you fondle crap, you not only get something on your fingers... you

33

*Nalli*

also end up flushing your awareness. Take out the trash, bring in
the clowns. Any votes for working on old cars?

**This is the "Button" section. It will discuss the search we make to find our "buttons" (aka motivation).**

How does a person unshackle the motive to work, to study, to exercise, to socialize, to fence with stress, to smile at losing, to include one more tango on an already busy dance card, or to put one more straw on the burdened camel's back? Can motive happen, if you simply say, "Shazam! It will be done!"?

Do addictions occur before or after a person's motivation has crashed and burned? Is it true that the initial part of everything is the most difficult and stressful? Can a person use a pep-talk to turn up the glow of motivation? Who pays the check when a person orders a triple shot of motivation? Is it safe to drive while motivated? Are enthusiasm and motivation twins? Are our emotions the "ground-zero" of our motivation chain?

Let's look at a definition and see where it leads us. <u>Motivation is attitude where commitment and interest join energy and action</u>. How is this attitude pumped? Darn, another question--where are the answers? We're in luck... because attitude is a human condition. We have attitudes that "paint" us positive, indifferent, or negative: He has a zit attitude. It's a town without an attitude. My cat has a cute attitude.

Which of these is best is not so obvious. Is a positive attitude <u>always</u> preferred to a negative attitude? And what exactly is an indifferent attitude--is this one of those oxymoronic word-combinations? It depends on the social outcome of the behavior influenced by the attitude. For example, I have a negative attitude (low motivation) about killing a person (self or others). This, to me, makes negative better here. Indifferent attitudes leave me turning slowly in the wind.

At issue in living a productively active waltz is lining up the appropriate motivation (attitude) in time and context. Motivation can vary from plus to minus with time and context. A successful steerage to a specific, desired <u>social</u> outcome is

35

guided by awareness of self. The emotional self, for example, is one of the aspects of "you," where attitude dwells.

The goals you set do not necessarily tell you of self, but <u>why</u> you set them does. Goals do not guarantee motivation. Goals, in themselves, do not motivate. Goals are contextual,.. they are part of the whole. People <u>do</u> living without aware goals; but people do <u>nothing</u> without motive. To be alive is to have motive. To set clear, attainable summits of social achievement is to be "good." It's additive to the collective "good," when you reach a social goal. To know that you've arrived at a pre-set point along your pathway, is encouraging. Apply energy in a smooth pace. Do not attempt to exceed your reach, and don't force your tempo. Stay within "self." As habit strengthens habit, so success nurtures success. Use small steps, and create social value for "goodness sake." Living "well" is a full-time proposition of investing self-knowledge in social and ecological ventures that result in generational abundance and quality.

Why discuss motivation in an exercises and games book? Without the attitude to match the time and context nothing <u>social</u> can occur on the path of living, which each of us create from moment-to-moment. Motivation constantly bumps into the standard question: "If not now, when? If not us (me), who?"

Now, is the time. And now moves with us as surely as our heartbeat does; neither goes away until we are dead. You (we) are the one(s). No one in the long, people-stuffed history of the global adventure has been better able to create <u>your</u> living path with a heart and dignity for you, than <u>you</u> are in this time and context.

A little is better than nothing when the issue is creating social or ecological value. And it's best to take a nibble, before you take a bite. Move at your own pace, set your own rhythm, but move! Creating opportunity and value with self, others and Nature is <u>important</u>. Be proud of any social or ecological effort, however small... and remember, <u>always</u> show-up tomorrow. Roust out the drones from the hive-site of your temperament.

Stay fit! Wellness is a person's best chance to deflect the arrows of fatigue and apathy. Fatigue is a voracious sump from which motivation is ill to find escape. Wellness is not just nice, it is necessary in the pursuit of creating the good life. Wellness has many enemies: neglect being big among these... with sleeplessness being, in my experience, the leader of the shaggy pack. Wellness includes the self in <u>all</u> of its aspects: "Free-weights in moderation are great for the body. What free-weights are you using for your spirit?"

Is all the pain and gain of physical training and growing just for temporary appearance? Time has a big eraser on its pencil when it comes to appearance. Time can and will diminish the shine of appearance--it's one of Nature's genetic totems.

Physical fitness and appearance are useful, and I do my part for myself. But people are living as adults almost twice as long today as people did a century ago. How do you intend to use the extra years when youthful appearance and reproduction of the species are no longer practical purposes? We need, as individuals, to become friends with our "heart and soul" (poetic terms that await your definitional dance) and to bring wellness and harmony to all the aspects of self. "Heart and soul" are cozy purring-terms to me... that have no age limits and reside in-and-between all aspects of self.

My friend Dave, knowing that poor sleep equates to low motivation, suggests avoiding sleep-interrupting, abstract thinking completely at bed-time. He prefers natural-mechanical thoughts in areas of special interest to him. For example, camping out, welding, carpentry, sailing, bureaucratic meetings, or even sleep itself (in nap form).

Oh, and how about the jumpy-body jitters? Reduce the chemicals use, and increase the daily muscle-involvement. Go for an evening walk, but leave the quart jug of double espresso at home. A well-spent, at-peace body rarely snubs an invitation to rest. Sleep aids, such as alcohol and pills are crutches, for the most part. The question that emerges from chronic use of such is: Which came first, the crutches or the crippleness? Many a garden-buff sleeps like a babe-in-the-buff following a work-out in the soil. I know one that absolutely purrs after transplanting a crepe myrtle or two.

"Bad nerves. I've got bad nerves," is an expression I've heard often (having been in the "bad nerves" business for a number of years) but never could isolate. The clinical "talk-shops" of America runneth over with bad nerves--but nobody, as far as I know, has ever seen one. Attitudes and excuses are often close cousins.

"Whistle while you whittle, boy. It'll calm the bad nerves," was told to me by an old porch-rocking neighbor man of my youth. What I've found is: whistling doesn't improve a person's skill to whittle (or to golf, ala Fuzzy Z.). What it does is help calm your attitude, keep you on task, and may save you a finger, or a stroke. A fellow called "Stumpy" said, "Never whittle when you're angry."

"Bad nerves" can be an anchor on social motivation. And as Sam Snead renown golfer, demonstrated in his later years on the golf course: The "yips" can destroy your "short" game in golf. The "yips" was Mr. Snead's "bad nerves" term for the demise of his putting skills. The "yips" can also occur in the creative game of living--especially when wellness fades.

Wellness is necessary for good performance, and is an excellent living-move choice. "Avoid extremes" is a well-tested and valid carry-over lesson from ancient Greece. With physical exercise, seek toning, don't try to fly to the moon; with the other aspects of self seek balance and harmony. How do you gauge this? Try awareness. I am not interested, for example, in leaving all my energy in the bed, the gymnasium, the mine-pit, the library, the marketplace, the barroom, the chapel, the schoolroom, at table, or on the pinnacle of K-2. Extremes are out there for one reason only--to be avoided.

You've heard mentioned the long running debate between--which came first--the reach or the grasp. Should your grasp exceed your reach, or vice versa? The quote: "...for why else is there a heaven?" is a vote for one's reach exceeding one's grasp. In goal attainment assure that you grasp the outcome you seek by exceeding the goal with "follow through." Take at least "three steps" past every goal. Run through the finish line tape (so to speak) of every goal, large, small, or tiny. Souls don't want to just get to heaven (reach), they want to get into heaven (grasp), once they get there (am I right?). Reach your goal, then grasp it through follow-through and impetus. Do not quit at the forward edge.

A nice finish to this section, it seems to me, would be to 1) Repeat the question: Why mention motivation in a book of awareness exercises and games? Followed by 2) My answer (an answer you may have shaped for yourself already). I believe that to think about human motivation is the purest of invitations across the threshold to self awareness in all its aspects. To discover human motivation is to answer the deep mysteries of human life, society, cultures, and close dancing. This is probably a feat far beyond our pale blush of wisdom--but an exercise well-worth practicing.

*Nalli*

## Some final tidbits:

Some people remember loved ones and past times through photographs, films and videos. Not a bad method, but I prefer daily behaviors, gestures and motions, such as starting the car, rinsing my face (as mentioned), a falling leaf, the smell of freshly mowed grass.

The reading of books, poems, newspapers (the comics and sports) is, for me, great relaxation. Holy Scripture is a favorite relaxant of many. Some printed stuff <u>is</u> my type, some <u>isn't</u>. I read the <u>is</u>, skip the <u>isn't</u>.

Some music <u>is</u>, some telephone chats, too.... But there are lotsa "ain't for me" in the stack.

Snap the trap of T.V. slavery. How? Shut off a favorite program--Now! Hit the power-switch right in the middle of the main course. The "burden relief" may be more comfortable by far then the dreaded anxiety of withdrawal. Try it, take a step on the path of a new direction. The T.V. habit makes me more tired than relaxed. Give yourself a treat, hit the switch... now and then.

My friend Bill says he puts each day on the track of his choice by looking out the bedroom window and saying, "Good morning, Morning." He says it in French. Is he talking "narrow guage" here? He and Voltaire might enjoy each other.

I've heard that there are people who create, compile, memorize, and rehearse a Personal Awareness Profile, to be used at cocktail parties to reply to the question, "Who are you?" This profile lists their favorite music, art, textures, colors, recipes, jokes, etc.,.. their sign of the Zodiac, political leanings, and their voting record--should they corner someone. As fads come and go they screen their rolodex of "Who am I" items--toss and add. This style is too compulsive and other-driven for my taste, but some "yuppie-boomers" swear by it.

But don't get me wrong. Lightening your load by getting rid of stuff, such as clothes or traits that not longer fit your body or your personality are great exercises in awareness. Holding an annual garage sale does more than put a little change in your jeans' pockets. It can be down-right liberating. And giving to people who can and will use your gifts is highly freeing. Try it! Be a volunteer! Be a coach! Be a mentor! Be a friend! Be a free-standing bell-tower!

For me shredding old files is an air-freshening activity of highest level for my mood. I've never understood the bureaucratic fascination with junk-papers. But, of course, I'm a fellow who enjoys "sharing" old clothes. Next week, my high school prom suit goes.

I need your help. I would appreciate any suggestions for taking the "boredom virus" out of clipping the nails on my fingers and toes. Forget the paper shredder, I will <u>not</u> use the shredder. Terror is not always awareness.

P.S. Was Dowd the name of the Jimmy Stewart character? "Elwood P." my brother-in-law Chuck assured me when I mentioned this postscript to him. Some people have the darnedest memories for the darnedest things. I'll have to ask Chuck about his trivia-memory exercises.

# Games

**Get in, get over, get under, get around, get through, get with, get out of: <u>the</u> game!  Which game?  Who's it?  What's on second?          Time-out, please.**

The game for living well is the game of AWARENESS.  The personal art of creating a path with a heart and dignity (a social and ecological path), of creating opportunity, value, humor, respect, patience, and productive activity is a full-time job of shelling peas and stirring the pot.  Awareness is what I enjoy writing about, what I enjoy doing.  Awareness reduces our moments served as hapless victims.

We create the good life and have fun in doing it, by doing it with others socially and with Nature.  The path to being on the inside of life's context of awareness is created in playing the game of "friendship."  But friends are never found without effort. Friends do not come ready-made waiting to be plucked from a shelf, a carton, a bottle, or a syringe.  The game of "friends" is a two-way creative act of sharing.

The grandest moments in living are found in "becoming a friend, being a friend, and remaining a friend."  This "tough-love" game of trust, honesty, and loyalty is based upon the premise that while a person can never have too many friends, one friend is surely enough to sustain a person right to the edge of time.

43

Have you ever had a friend? Ever been one? If yes, then you are in the game. If no, then come on, get in the game! Everyone is welcome. The arena is as big as life itself, and haste is neither a necessary, nor a needed trait here. Age is not a limiter. Prejudice, however, is. Prejudice is a fear-run game full of "cut-offs and not-listening."

The games and activities witnessed in a society reflect the principles, values, and fundamental standards of those who live in and create that society. Historically, games have been conceived and designed to reflect living events and human skills as honored by the society of origin. A society's games can enhance, hone, and train, not merely the game's graces, but the grander scale of human graces in living... if they are permitted to do so through full public participation (not spectating only).

In our stress-burdened, distraction-addicted society we have turned the cat inside-out... and now we wonder why it walks and purrs so weirdly. But it should come as no surprise--our games reflect us and our living. We made our games from what we were, and we modify them to what we are. Teamwork reflects social quality and pride; selfishness reflects fear and insecurity. Anyone interested in a little teamwork in day-to-day exchanges, for a change of pace? I am! Look for my lantern, give me a "shout."

The game of "complain and blame" is played by many because, since they have not yet figured-out how to create opportunity (relate) and value (share), it gives them a voice to claim pain and fame. Prejudice, in any form, is a main character in this game. The objective of the game is to step on someone else's throat and crush the beauty from their purpose of being. This allows the "winner" to imagine that he/she stands an inch or two taller as she/he struggles to peer out of the latrine of his/her existence. Them/they lose.

"I cannot live without beauty," said Camus. On some streets that I've walked, Camus would have died instantly. I feel about beauty much the same as Camus did, which is why I weaken in mood around some people. Their approach to living seems such an ugly game to me. In most cities I've stopped asking for "a room with a view."

Some people are masters at discovering the unpleasant, being abusive, and nursing the negative. They unload a carping-burden of selfish purpose upon all they touch. The "ugly,.. isn't life awful" game says, "I cannot live <u>with</u> beauty." Some game, huh? Ever play it? I play it far more often than I like. "Seeing the ugly" is an attitude I need to work out of my system. As Churchill said, "Any damn fool can see what's wrong with it. What's right with it?"

How can the habit of the "ugly" game be broken? Spend more time with people you enjoy, in places you enjoy. This has been my birthday resolution and annual wish for the past several years now. I find it is a good destination, within my reach, and certainly within my grasp. A forum of friends is far more nourishing in this pursuit than is a forum of "lovers." Ask some of our recent, more-immature Presidents, et. al.

To add a little spice of calm, spend some time alone. Alone-time has been a familiar condition with many creative "doers." Productive activity can occur in groups numbered from one to infinity... so too can humor, patience, and respect. If "beauty is a joy," then do you also believe that "joy can be beautiful"? Do you believe that "a person can be alone in a crowd?" How about "being in a crowd when alone?"

The "old proverbs" game. Due to the low-activity, passive behavior level of many people today Mother Nature is not the headmistress of our daily living school as she once was. The ad-person on television has far more influence on our daily attitudes, direction, and fad-dashes than any time-worn maxims of Nature. My generation may have been the last to have been raised purely on natural adages, such as the "spilled milk" tale, or "eggs in one basket," etc. Aesop and his tail-less fox fade into a fable-dom of Babel-dom.

This "old proverbs" game is not as popular in current, media-driven times when vicarious and virtual learning till and steer youthfull minds. Natural maxims do not carry meaning, because we are now light-years' warriors and electronic-circuits' technocrats busily engaged in our starships "Denial" and "Contradiction." Does the saying about sweat, perspire, and glow say anything to you, e.g.? How about fences, green grass, small dogs, and razor-blades?

The old comparisons today serve more to confuse than to instruct. It appears that only basic bathroom behavior, body odors, sex, and bad breath are widely recognized as natural. Human sexual stuff is passed in inflated reality as having special heavenly qualities, exceeded only by good pizza. So, should you wish to play any "proverbs" games with companions you might choose something to do with the toilet, personal smells, animal rutting, or halitosis mints. Natural is rather plastic these days.

Isolation can be a friend as well as a foe. "Isolation" is a game we cannot avoid, now and then. Embrace and dance with your isolation. Let it be a motive, not a burden. Don't let isolation rush you into mistakes. If relating errors occur, then cozy up to them slowly. Get to know the members of the Mistake family, and keep track of what dark part of the woods Mr. or Ms. Wrong is leading you. Don't waste energy by trying to right the past, know <u>where</u> you are... and patiently (don't rush in either direction) start moving awarely forward along humor, respect, and productive activity's path. Mistakes are full of <u>if's</u>, while the good life is full of <u>do's</u>. To avoid a life-time of foul balls create a yellow brick road of productive activity.

We play our games and live our lives as <u>if</u> they were deadly contests between a cobra and a mongoose. Such battles have only one winner and no pleasure for the loser. When the alarmed call "The Mistake family is at hand!" rattles us awake, the cold shadow of stress crawls, dives, burrows into our beds. Icy toes rip at our dreams as we cry, "God, I hate this Isolation madness." Some awareless mis-adventures in living can leave us deep in the fear-filled woods of Despair. This part of the woods doesn't offer a lot of positive choices, there's much sobbing at night, nobody returns phone calls, and there's always "hell-served-for-breakfast."

We need to bring the social joy of living into the competitive spirit of games rather than bring the competitive spirit of games to the social exchanges of our daily affairs. Our games must be shaped to reflect and model and honor the cooperative values that we know are essential to an effective society. We tend to pretend that group living came <u>after</u> the invention of games. Today our living performance, too often, reflects the competitive distress driven by selfish personal achievement needs. We need, at this point in social development, games that enhance and nourish self-aspects' fitness and cooperation. Which team do you prefer: Isolation or community? Your life. Your choice. Your game.

Of people there are those loved, those despised, the noble, the common, the proud, the profane, the good, the bad, the truthful, the dishonest, the altruistic, the self-interested, the wise, the foolish, the lefties, the righties, the <u>usw</u>, the etc. In the game of "un-monopoly in living" which words do you choose from moment-to-moment for you to be recognized as?

Because there are so many points of view in the shaded marketplaces, meadows, bowling alleys, and back alleys of living, everything, as decided by someone, has some purpose in it. Why else would people do the things they do? For example, if you were to accidentally eat the wash water for soup--it is not soup, as you will doubtlessly determine before you finish your second bowl full, but it is warm and it will certainly take your mind off your hunger for a while (or so you might explain to laughing associates between retches). In creating the step-by-step game of "opportunity" don't settle for less than the real thing or the right stuff. "Be aware!" is the ante of those who make winning choices. How do you define: winning? Good choices remove the need for weak explanations. How do you define: good? How do you define: good win?

The game of "being burned-out ashes, singe, or toast," which entails the art of using numbing, exaggerated auto-ism in all conversation, comes to the game board when a boring person joins a neurotic depressive on a skate board to nowhere. This game emphasizes that an important part of living is getting through the draggy innings of self-absorption. The recommended remedial booster-series is creating humor, respect, patience, and productive activity. The Catch-18 is: the Bore and the Depressive have to contribute mutually. "Ashes, ashes, we all fall down."

The "Shoemaker" definition of burn-out fits well here: "Burn-out comes when others do not do their part in preparing the burrito. Ole`!" This is also known as: Trickle-down dumping of responsibility without any consensus, or authority. Teachers, e.g., burn-out, singe, or toast when the school principal is a bum (a wannabe superintendent), or when parents provide only genetics, abuse, and social ignorance (wannabe say-whats). Some parents' only willing contribution to their children are the initial "body fluids."

Burn-out and its by-products can occur on any team, with any age level, status, or lifestyle. The victims of this game honor despair. The survivors believe that the solution for deep occupational, conversational, or personal/sexual burn-out (after romance takes a hike) is to hide in a "cave," become your own dearest boss, colleague, companion, do it all yourself. Most stop short of becoming an impoverished monk or nun with a vow of chastity, of course. Body fluids do have a vote. The smell of burn-out can be found in every city, town, nook, and cranny. If you ever find yourself, or others, at "ash-down," the step following melt-down, I recommend: no deep inhaling, no close dancing. Prayer is the invention of choice here. Turn-up your awareness slowly, gradually, continuously, and stay away from all invitations to visit any "armpit," yours or others. There are no winners in this game of burnout.

"Trivial Pursuit" is not just a popular board game for den and kitchen, it's the current American way of living. Most of us say, "If it's trivial, I'll pursue it. If it's kinky trivia, I'll pursue it on all fours. The trivia is afoot, Watson!" Many Americans live in a daily mental/emotional/spiritual space-locker somewhere between "Gone with the Wind" and "The Regis and Kathie Lee" show.

The treadmill of trivial pursuit in our daily affairs has us addicted to our fears and put us on a narrow pathway to oblivion. Does anyone know of this addiction? Oh, indeed they do. Politicians know it well... and they "play," not to our courage and strengths, to our fears and insecurities. Insurance companies, the Pentagon, medical and psychological groups, religious institution, educational associations, international business moguls, con-agents of every stripe, lottery games,.. does the list have an end? "Trivial Pursuit! Oh, can I play?" we cry. "You bet," comes the chorus of replies from the Cheshire-cat crowd, "but you have to furnish your own barf bags."

To gain a finger hold on awareness start by making some lists.

1) List your addictions, e.g., electricity, cars, caffeine, soft TP (2 ply), hot showers, sleep. Some people are down-right giddy over amperes and volts. Their favorite odor is ozone. And then others are giddy over clipping their toenails.

2) List your habits and reflex responses. Please define the word habit as you know it. Is habit picking your fingers when nervous? Or is daily jogging a habit? And what is a reflex response in your world? Is shaking hands with others a reflex action? Or is uncontrollable laughter when your car breaks down on inner-city gang turf at 2:00 a.m. such a response?

3) List your fears. "Free yourself up" by being aware of the chains that hold you, the urges that direct you, the impulses that control you. The idea in this is to sort your motives into small piles; they're easier to recognize that way. If living is, in fact, a process of relating and sharing, knowing why you stuck your nose into a certain armpit-situation, and knowing why you chose to leave

49

your nose in that specific armpit for so long... can be useful: if not to you, then to those who try to diagnose you and talk you down from the ledge.

Let me ask you a question. Is the word <u>relating</u> too overused and polluted in meaning? How about the word <u>sharing</u>? Is it clearer to say: A person <u>participates</u> in eating, in sex, in voting, in being, in family,.. in the living process,.. rather than to use the words <u>relate</u>? <u>share</u>?

In order to relate, share, <u>or</u> participate in the game of "aware living" how you understand the words and terms that influence your thoughts, actions, and beliefs is a key motive for social change and direction, plus or minus, that you select?

Do people relate and share in "road rage," addiction-surrender, suicide? or do they participate? Maybe a major glitch in our

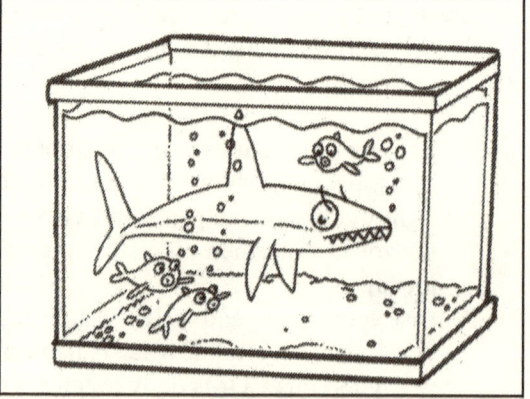

social-flow today is: too much <u>participating</u>, and not enough <u>relating</u> and <u>sharing</u>. Have apathy and reflexive indifference taken the high-ground over social/ecological awareness and self-enrichment? Egad! A shark may be in the aquarium.

I recently read (a note of mine, I think), "Acceptance of relating breaks the neurotic barriers in living." Sounds okay, huh? Does it tell you anything? I don't understand it... and substituting the word <u>participating</u>, for relating, doesn't help me a whit. I find it interesting how, in dulled awareness, we so quickly bite on empty bait. Don't chase the wrong bait. A diet of practiced stupid-awarelessness does not help the small fry become a big fish.

Perhaps if a person would pursue understanding through the aware creating of humor, patience, respect, and productive activity, rather than seek perfection, then words would have an applied meaning and purpose. Terms, such as acceptance, recognition, relating, sharing, participating, etc. would then serve to reduce anxiety and distress rather than increase them. It's worth a step. Why not? Why stay locked in the penalty box of ignorance? The "I hear you, but my lack of experience causes your words to confuse me" is a tired game. No Tally ho! or Get in the hunt! on that weary trail, for sure. There is not much future swimming in a shark-filled aquarium, even if you're a shark.

Who said, "Newspapers never print any good news"? Whenever I run short of encouragement as I'm stirring in the recipe ingredients for a tasty day, I borrow a cup or two from my neighbors. By knocking on their front-door? No, by reading the wedding and birth announcements in a local newspaper. This "cup full of sugar" game helps the "front page" go down. I wish them wellness and a good journey, and I hope they choose to relate and share, rather than just participate and use.

Each game has a specific set of rules which define that particular game as it differs from any other game. If you don't play using a game's specific rules, absolutely, then you are not playing the game as <u>defined</u> by its rules. You're playing another altered, diverse game. No two people that I know play the game of golf, for example, using the same rules.

Some people break and bend (change) the rules of games--golf is a common victim. Some players are such habitual "changers" of the rules in golf, they even deceive themselves. To be permitted to say that you performed at a particular level in a game, you cannot simply melt and vary the rules to fit your whim or your vanity. When you "flush" the rules that define a game,.. then you're playing another game with different wild cards. In golf, this may help explain why many local club "aces" aren't on the Tour.

A local wag once told me, "You'll find more liars in a small-town golf-course club house than in the confessional box at St. Peter's in Rome." I've also found liars to be rather thick in the marketplaces, businesses, and homes of America. To deceive in interacting with others is to abort and avoid sharing. A person who deceives and lies cannot relate and share in the same moment. In the game of "lie detection" when you sense deception don't give off a loud BEEP!, just smile softly and check to see who's not playing by the rules as you understand them. Being "It" is not where you want to be. Rules-translation is exactly why it is necessary for us to have courts and judges. But so many? Are we that unclear about the "games" we are, and are not, playing?

In looking at this society's balance scales between information and experience the scales today tip sharply in the direction of information. We've been told, "Information is power," and "talk" media/entertainment/politics flood our every sensory channel and sneak into every orifice too stupid to pucker or run. So what exactly are the "rules" of the Power Game? Why does it seem that whenever the "Power-brokers" of government, industry, and assorted bureaucratic institutions play "La Game," we, the "informed" public, take it in the shorts? Are we "playing" on different fields, using different rules and terms? Are we, the "informed" public, really players, or are we merely the pain-bearers? If we, the people, aren't players in this Democratic Republic,.. what are we? Would you read me the Rules, one more time?

Information is useless without positive application; and positive application is basically non-existent, without experience. Currently, our schools charge us huge sums of money to widen the gap between our information and our applied-living skills. Could they be thinking that "information stuffing" alone is education? Can social-quality stand the gaff of the "profit-taking" madness? "Close the gap" is an awareness game that promotes a balance between learning and performance. The role of positive social models, critical players in this game, is to show us how to sort the wheat from the chaff in the harvest of information and experience. Are you seeking education and settling for information? Are you seeking a creative life and settling for a passive existence? Play "close the gap!" Don't play: Close your mind, close your life.

To associate with some people is far worse than no associations at all. To believe that <u>anything</u> is better than <u>nothing</u> (loneliness) can be emotional suicide. Have you noticed? The "rock and the hard place" is a tough game. A game that doesn't take prisoners, or give lifts to hitchhikers. Sort your cards carefully, and do not let desperation, or fatigue dull your awareness. In some situations, when you evaluate the alternatives, <u>nothing</u> is perfect.

"Emotional war" games, once the exclusive energy drain of the leisure class, have migrated and trickled down through the sweat-seams to all classes of people (in our classless society, yet). Emotional-war skirmishes often result in crippling casualties. These "ambush and run" tactics are engaged in from the arboretum to the zoo, by assholes to zealots, rich or poor.

These emotional/neurotic games of daily destruction are nourished by a broad-scope fantasy of great personal and familial expectations, poor individual awareness match-ups, and your basic spoiled immaturity. It sounds as if we're describing the recipe of a popular television soap opera, does it not? Well, neurotic trickle-down and cross-pollination have to come from somewhere... and the TV pulp-mill is an excellent "somewhere," when one thinks about Emotional War Games.

Put passion into every action and every thought if you want to join the dance called the "wild and crazy world" game. Learn to stroll with an air of happy success and you will sweep the board over the odds of passive failure. Passion, well ladled, gives you control during the difficult gaffs and transitions in <u>living</u>, such as joining and separating, beginnings and endings,

53

starts and stops, the comings and goings... and in <u>dying</u>. Passion is a marvelous companion both in private and in public.

Each person, excepting sports announcers, has limited natural-passion fuel. Here enters the need for the invention of the double-espresso bar and the corner "coke" dealer. Keep your passion-tank in mind and use awareness in selecting your stool at the "careers'" counter. Having only one butt to use at a time, it's possible, but awkward (and at times rude), to occupy more than one space at a time.

Be advised: Anger is not the only passion. (Color me Red!). Sensitivity is a passion, joy is a passion, affection is a passion, creativity is a passion (Color me Pastel! if you like). Use passion in living just as an artist uses color in painting, or a writer uses nouns, verbs, adjectives, and adverbs. Use passion to give expression to the spirit of being alive and creatively curious. Put some energy into the "passion" game, it's a good investment.

Declare yourself "happy" periodically during your day... and dare the world to join you. We too often suffocate our personal and social interactions with overexposure and continuous, lengthy togetherness. Keep all visits brief, productively comfortable, and fun. We tend to overindulge our fear of isolation and our discomfort with loneliness. To couple, or group-up to excess can result in an acute migraine of emotional hang-over; a case of double loneliness and crowd-burden. Joy blooms when we're with others in Nature's greenhouse creating a pathway of balance and harmony. The seeds of joy are our awareness of self. These seeds require liberal doses of personal culling for best results in creating your personality of choice. Don't expect to scatter "crap" seeds, if you seek to create "velvet-stemmed" roses, FCOL.

# Let's end this section with some games and notions that can influence awareness through mental stirring.

For me socially fun games provide a challenge, allow random creativity, humor and quality time involvement on a reasonably level field of play. Social games cannot be played by your average lonesome dove, short of severe boredom. My list includes: Scattergories, Scrabble, Trivial Pursuit, Balderdash, Fictionary Dictionary, and Foreign Language Cusswords Crosswords.

Awareness activities that I've enjoyed, or watched others enjoy, include: Writing of letters, cards,.. books, term papers (no, scratch that one), hokey horoscopes,.. even fortune notes for popcorn boxes, and hooter tattoo messages, tai chi, reading, knitting, chess, juggling, math problems and posers, checkers (Chinese and cracker-barrel), darts, cooking,.. making endless lists, such as this one... and shouting: "Somebody stop me!"

A final activity of special fascination to me is: Words and languages. I can spend every recess on the merry-go-round of words, their origins and related idioms. Of course, going for a walk with a friend is nice, too. Oh, and how about breathing, that's got some major pluses... especially on a fresh spring day. Have you ever asked: Why are games invented, why are they played? Are we nurturing inquiry or avoiding boredom? Are players of popular or personal-private games more aware and more peaceful than the average apple? or are they as lonely as a southwest desert wind? Is self discovery and exploration the only true game in the history, geography, and creation of human living?

*Nalli*

## A Final Games tidbit.

Is there anything to the Hackers and Internet Cruising Game? Is there any self-awareness-gain potential here, or is this just a curious trek into an information sewer maze? Will knowledge and understanding survive all this stalking and mugging behavior? And does anybody, in this speed of light, megabyte world, care? Oh, by the way, are modems electronic condoms that work in both directions, or what? Any informational virus control here? It is not only okay to do so, but it is recommended that you "talk to your-self" about such cross-flow. What "informational compost" will do the most to assist you in creating the Self of your choice? Be productively active, observe the results,.. tell a friend: It's Game Time!

*Nalli*

# Set Your Own Rhythm!

If you aren't going to take charge of your life,.. who is? If you won't take control of your world,.. who will? If you choose not to set your own rhythm,.. will some control weirdo plunge into the vacuum for you? Are you willing to risk it? It is your life, your world, your rhythm... and you only get one of each... at any one moment. Awareness puts fear on the run. Join the chase, rout the rascal... set your own rhythm! (Doo-dah, doo-dah!)

Some people would have you believe the title for the Guidebook to a Good Life is "Written on the Sky," in huge, clear letters. This is a notion proceeding from a stress-oppressed brain, body, and spirit. Such a book is a sham. The notion that living and dying are pre-set steps, controlled by set-in-concrete laws, laws, and more laws that each person <u>must</u> follow, honor, and experience without pause, hitch, blink, reflection, change, or omission is balderdash and bird-droppings. Do not confuse <u>Life</u> and <u>Death</u> for, or with, <u>Living</u> and <u>Dying</u>. There is a vast difference between the bookends and the book, you may have noticed--I certainly have. Choice occurs <u>inside</u> the binders, not on the outside. Choices are the grapes of your Rhythm-Setting Wine, cultivate and tend them well.

Nothing is so written on the sky about your living, your productive activity, your rhythm as to be outside the edit of choice. Nor are there such things of indelible certainty written on the wind, nor on the bathroom wall's at Skeet's Drive Inn Restaurant, nor on the warmth of a young gallant's smile,.. nor on the hem of an ingenue's skirt.

We each live. We each

die. We each measure the means and the beat, we each meter the try and the dare. No <u>one</u> goal is pre-set in the style and grace, balance and tempo of living and dying as the single ideal suited for all. No two things are identical in Nature's nest. Now <u>that</u>,... you might find written on the sky, the wind, or a wall. No two human "hearts" set the same identical rhythm. We all play, in unique and special ways, our individual instrument of living and dying. As members in life's orchestra our mission is to create a concerted social and ecological tempo of balance and harmony. When tempo is erratic, the cost is HUGE.

The rules we honor from past generations are those directives which have proven useful in leading to social morality and cooperative behavior. Thou shall make war, or be hateful, or fear-soaked, or riskless, or without personal rhythm... are not now, nor have they ever been universally popular mandates for living at the upper reaches of human potential. Is the song of human poetry mostly in praise of: rhythm, or chaos? peaceful productive activity, or war-ful destruction?

Is the idea of awareness-rhythm new? Hardly. Other centuries have urged the choice, in verse, song, prayer, proverb, promise, praise, and parental whispers to cherished children, to seek health, community, happiness, cooperation, wisdom, radiance, wholesomeness, harmony, and creativity. Today, our anxieties have us spinning frantically in the wind of Greed's foul breath. Greed creates no community, and it heeds too many masters and sirens: it never finishes a dance, the Three Ravens-- Fear, Loneliness, and Pollution--all sing in the extreme choice- key of Greed. This is not a pretty sound.

Ample are the historic advisories to focus wisely on balance and harmony. Choices need, through awareness, to be sorted into cause, purpose, direction, and consequence. To rush to judgment, to haste to rage are fretful, peevish, foolish, and unbearably light-headed and ill-hearted. Some examples of past warnings are: "The hound that chases many foxes at once will catch only the scented air." "He who builds to every man's advice will have a crooked house." This Danish proverb sounds a lot like the English proverb: "Too many cooks spoil the broth." "A dance happens one step at a time" and "Too many partners makes for madness." These words caution that to try to dance to more than one tune at a time will end in the dreaded Triple

Threat of "fumble, fart, and fall down." This jesting corrective was yelled long ago by a high school football coach at a person to remain unnamed. None of these warnings praise the absence of information, knowledge, or understanding--rather they cast their votes for the value of mature responsibility and a personal leadership of balanced and harmonious choices in creating one's path with a heart and dignity: forget the extremes.

George Bernard Shaw gave us a quote about awareness and courage in living. What he had to say was: "The power of accurate observation is commonly called cynicism by those who have not got it." What do you make of that? Would you be interested in inviting Mr. Shaw to breakfast? My guess is that he liked his eggs over <u>hard</u>, over <u>very</u> hard.

Carlyle (an incorrigible pessimist) said, "... and if I am in search of pain, I cannot go wrong." Pessimists enjoy, despite their claim that nothing matters, being right... and being miserable. What a map to the future, huh? "Show me the way to pain... and more pain, please. The twin peaks of my joy." Carlyle had a rhythm that I'll pass on. Did he, perhaps, time-travel and read your autobiography... or what?

On a more up-beat scale, Ralph Waldo Emerson wrote to us:

"With the key of the secret he marches faster from strength to strength, and for night brings day;
    While classes or tribes, too weak to master the flowing conditions of life, give way."

This is about the difference in self-reliant individuals and that greater crowd of folks who accept a weak personal rhythm which says," ...give way." We all come to this choice point-- remember the ol' "To be or not to be"? Which will be your direction and pace? You already possess the "key of the secret." Will you use it? Or will you lose it?

In our youthful haste for a pillar of assurance we lasso an unsteady Humpty Dumpty. By this, I mean that we seek to live using a borrowed philosophy and unquestioned values. We start our climb up the faces of the blocks of life's challenges seeking to build our personal pyramid. Most of us master walking, talking, and potty-training, but how many of us learn the skills for making balanced and harmonious choices? Controlled desk-behavior and compliance in classroom mechanics are not enough. Our incessant blurring of cause with correlation shows an awareness-poor diet.

Praying that all will go well, we proceed with a growing uncertainty: Is our anchor solid? Are our values' stanchions secure? Is our unquestioned and borrowed philosophy flexible and permissive of inquiry and creativity?

Our Humpty wiggles, it wobbles, it rocks, and it teeters... and at times it falls. If it does topple, guess upon whom this unstable Humpty will Dumpty. Old Mother Hubbard won't be the target, nor will the Three Mice. So, who is next in line?

The acknowledged greats of history are those who set their own rhythm, <u>most</u> of the time. Rhythm setting, as a personal choice, is a major factor in a person's ecological and social effectiveness and well-being in living.

We cannot see what gravity, or electricity is. Yet we know how to produce and use the latter, and we can witness the effect of the former. When someone tells you, "Since you cannot see the resultant "good feelings" of social cooperation, it is foolish to seek it." Don't be convinced. To learn what produces harmony and balance in living, and how to create this magical effect of the self are primary forces in my daily living. As we have learned to use electricity, despite that most of us have no idea what it is, I want to put the power of social cooperation and ecological dignity to full use in creating better moments for self, and others, and Nature in my daily affairs. The good feelings <u>are</u> real--I recently visited with one. I named it Laura... after my first granddaughter. Mother Nature is keenly interested in this creative dance. She just slipped me a note.

Put events into your life that advise you to flow rather than to jerk. Awareness of the signs of exhaustion is necessary for continuous, effective pace to occur. Thinking, e.g., is best done with a comfortable steady pace to glide and guide along. Try a pathway of Balance and Harmony,.. see if your "thinking" time doesn't increase, become more humorous, and more productive. Try it for four or five years, I believe you'll like it. Burn-out, which favors silent ambush over bells and bugles, feasts upon the frantic, herky-jerky, I've-got-to-get-it-done-yesterday personality. How fast can you listen? How fast can you think? At what rate-range of living are you most respectful, productively active, patient, humorous, and aware? When are you in your health-zone? When are you not?

The person who seeks to walk a high wire is well-advised to tend to his step and to his pace. High ambition can become low disappointment in a hurry, when rhythm "sucks."

Personality is a social-behavioral term, an awareness verb in noun's clothing. Personality is defined relative to a person's inter-personal cooperative skills, energy expression, and dance rhythm. Mother Nature see us as suicidal.

Relating and sharing--the demonstration and performance of one's created personality--are the essence of being, doing, and living. Discovering and creating who you are is a life-long adventure--it starts early, ends late. The music and the step of your dance on life's stage are yours to create, monitor, and adjust. The street named Self is life long... right up until the final, tiny bulb goes out.

A stress-management "expert" I know (his colleagues call him Dr. Jitters) once said, "Anxiety junkies seek stimulation in the vise of external stress. The two plates of the vise are Ignorance and Stupidity; the results can be crushing, but they're rarely boring." In the exchange of anxiety for boredom, these "edge-walkers" seem to confuse pounds and ounces, prevention and cure. Dr. Jitters, who makes his living wages from "stress casualties," said to avoid the vise, we each need to recruit and train our own productively active drummer. Good morning, Mr. Thoreau, how's your drummer today? Still depressed?

Since, unlike in Mr. Thoreau's time, there are no longer stress-free beds lining the folds in Mother Nature's apron at nearby Walden Pond we can neither run, nor can we hide. Ignorance, stupidity, drugs, money, extremes-assorted have proven to be poor havens. Our best possibility is to mount a friendly, humor-supported counterattack against all rules and regulations, policies and procedures, ideas and notions that assail ecological and social harmony, balance, and sanity. Who chose this "beat?" Who's playing it? Who's dancing to it?.. and why?

"The proof of the pudding is (indeed) in the tasting" ...and, each spoonful will validate, or reject issues and steps along your journey, if you have the courage, vision, and energy to set your own rhythm. Do not accept spit and snot as sugar and spice. Reality is a creative responsibility of each of us. A society reflects the collective realities of the individuals. Can a society be insane? Of course. Can the entire planet be insane? We seem to be trying to determine that, don't we.

When you <u>know</u> the dance is a rumba, don't let anyone, even an experienced egg-sucker, convince you that it's a waltz. Hup! Toup! Three! Fo!.. Cha, cha, cha!.. Doodah, doodah! Please, don't eat the flowers... as in your or in your date's corsage. Make your moments <u>special</u>. A person who does the creative-moment doesn't have to rely on the Kodak Moment for rich memories.

The comment by Bertolt Brecht: "There goes the mob,.. and I must follow them, for I am their leader" will not be found hanging in the work-place of a rhythm-setter, except in jest. A person of self-set rhythm may smile, recognize that Mr. Brecht composed it as wit, not as wick, and even, perhaps, pass it to friends. Such messages of rhythm-less despair are the primary grist of "modem-ized," one-note bureaucrats who learn their "social" philosophy from rappers, rock singers, and printed coffee mugs. They not only think such messages are funny, they think they are <u>true</u> and <u>accurate</u>. Their prison has no walls, no guards... just Fax machines and PC's.

"A prisoner, in whatever cage contained, is never free" is a simple proposition about self and rhythm-setting. If a person stays in a situation as a prisoner by a choice based upon insecurity and fear, freedom's bloom is rarely smelled. Wishing does not break bars, and drugs, denial and distractions do not breach walls. May I remind you that Fool's Paradise <u>is filled with fools</u>. It's owned by fools, it's operated by fools, and it's "E-mail" is controlled by fools.

When a person walks in the rain, no one can readily see his/her tears. To hide the tears completely a good soaking is required. If you are sad in a sad crowd, no one there will likely take much notice. They're all too busy with being sad. Sad is an isolating event. But when it's your mood of choice, enjoy it! Glad, an interactive rhythm with others or Nature, is also a mood of choice; so, when you dance with Glad, enjoy it!

65

When a person is glad in a glad crowd is the result additive, or negatory? I've long believed: If you want to be sad, don't go to the party. Don't try to "pee" on the context-parade created by others. Set your own rhythm. Choose the mood and context you want to embrace, and, in its moment, enjoy it. By the way, in your experience, what effect of control does sad have on glad? and glad have on sad? Ever watch that tempo-struggle? Are we talking here about each person's contribution in creating context? Or are we talking about the influence of the many upon the few, the few upon the many? Tell me again, please, who is in charge? The rule is: "The dealer names the game." So, deal, or "pass the buck." Flip Wilson's Devil is waiting to dance. Or not. Some people like to "bebop," others prefer to "blame."

The individualist, poet Walt Whitman wrote to us: "I crowd your sleekest and best by simply looking toward you." Then he added: "With the hush on my lips I wholly confound the skeptic." I like the lines. I'm still trying to decide what I think of Mr. Whitman. I expect Mr. Whitman won't adjust his rhythm one way or the other, whatever I conclude. He's dead, you know. Another famous dead person is added to my "Invite to Breakfast" list.

As we engage on the playing field of life, most of us endlessly seek to define and delineate the boundary lines. What's foul? What's fair? A Book of Rules about family, daily conduct, marriage, a job, an education, how much fat to eat, when to draw to an inside straight, or what type pet is an ideal horoscopic energy-mate has been a historical human guest. Gurus, prophets, law-makers, pastors, coaches, mavens, evangelists, mentors, stockbrokers, teachers, sheeple-herders, ad-agents, song-writers, greasy-spoon menus, camp-directors, card-sharks, counselors, bookies, bartenders,... even consultants and motivational speakers... Wow! Hit a tree, Nalli. Stop!.. have been followed eagerly, even galloped after blindly. We hope, we pray, that others will set-the-rules, make-the-choices, and define the lines-of-play for us. When you have a referee, you have someone to <u>BLAME</u>. But individual Choice always decides whether you'll dance with a devil, or a saint today... now or later.

We chant, "I play to do it well. My best is all I have to give,.. and give... and give." We limp along, tripping over a weakened sense-of-humor and a flagging rhythm. We say we want to play the game well, but we rarely practice witnessed effectiveness, or create, when the breaks are going against us, a fresh pace and style. We move from crisis-ditch, to tear-soaked hankie, to stress-pot, to scar-tissue without so much as a grin, or an inch of creative change. Talk about "where are the grits?" Indeed, where <u>are</u> the grits? The Game of Scapegoat has no time-outs, no winners,.. not even any contenders. Mr. Whitman you are definitely crowding my sleekest and pinching my best.

Speaking of pinches, do you carry one pair of shoes through life trying to wedge them on to every pair of feet (situation) you meet? Magical slippers create no romantic endings on the dance floor of Elmtown, U.S.A. Creative flexibility is the sneaker size of smart choice in our dip and glide reality. Redream your dance. Dreams are well known for having elastic seams. "One size fits all" is fairy-tale thinking, mostly. By the way, have you driven a dream recently? Put a saddle on a mustang dream... and ride it, if you dare. Wahoo!

If you try to level every mountain peak that appears on the horizon of your life's view, you'll become a weary admirer of mediocrity, and you'll never reach a summit that exceeds the average. What's wrong with that? Nothing, if you believe the line... "Dreams do not require leveling, they simply require climbing" is just so much silly-putty and has no place on a peg in the cupboard of your awareness. Rhythm setting and dream riding are issues of choice. "Deal, or pass the buck!" says your Context.

Many people give up their dreams at the first splash of rising water, mild tremor, or peer/parent/pony/pal discouragement. When I was eighteen years old, I was told, one of the town drunks gave me the sermonette, "You'll give up your dreams soon enough now." Well, here I stand on my life's path some 3

X 18 plus a few years and my dreams are still a daily companion of mine. I have never accepted the quicksand-notion that to dream is done only by the "smart-asses" and the "weird-crazies." I admit to some desperate moments, but I'm still in the saddle. I encourage you: Don't watch your dreams from afar; don't chase them, ride them.

Our society, in its current free-fall pins and stripes, does not welcome, or warmly embrace the "serious" dreamer, the out-of-stepper, the individual who snatches-up the drumsticks and plays his/her own beat. Why? Such people can influence change, and the idea of deliberate change is a "no-no." The pipeline and the marketplace want straight-line, predictable, somewhat anxious, highly controllable, indebted consumers and users. In some societies it's impossible to tell the addictions from the despair, the benefits from the burdens, the solutions from the problems. When the "bottom line" dictates the march "beat," social coma is never far back in the parade. Change is far less dangerous to a society than is the restriction of new choices. The major threat to a society is: old ignorance. A changeless society stales to collapse. Confront ignorance with education, not with the fearful restriction of change and freedom of choice. Somebody spur me! I'm on an eraser, and the "bottom line" bromides are my "target of rub."

A society--the moment-to-moment beliefs, actions, and motives of all its members--that too long trains that the status quo is Zeus will fail. "It can't get any better than this" is a dead-end jingle. Without the light, vision, and fresh air of change created by enduring individual-dreams a society can neither stir its pudding, nor taste it. It becomes a small patch on History's undershorts, not a path with a heart and dignity influenced by productively active and humorous dreams.

Nightmares and dreams both cast intriguing shadows on the walls of a person's imagination and purpose. Loneliness, for example, in its nightmarish robes, has caused many a person to linger in a rancid pit of mis-mating. A sick bonding with Mr. or Ms. Wrong will turn youthful dreams of a romantic grace into nightmares of a narrow hell, quick-time. Forget the dark allure of this ritual, go early from such rhythm and don't look back at that dance floor. "Rituals are comforting," John Irving told us. "Rituals combat loneliness." So, why leave? Comforting, yes. Combat, maybe, John, but only temporarily. Rout and defeat, no: This is the role of relationship, not of ritual. Ritual and the status quo are kissing kin, and change is rarely invited to the party.

The person who refuses to honor abuse as either a gift, or as a duty, and who chooses not to give up the productive activity of creating her dreams will discover the peace of balance and harmony. In order to respect the past a person must have dreams for the future--otherwise the balance-arm snaps, the living adventure falls. Once a person discovers the creative joy of living with harmony and balance the smoke and mirrors of excessive materialism are no longer necessary. The rhythm of self-awareness brings the clarity of creative social and ecological cooperation and dignity.

A true measure of joy in living is found in translating your dreams into your social and ecological reality. The aware, thinking person--the person who casts his ballot for and guides on respect, humor, patience, and productive activity--early reaches the knowledge point that his future does not exist as might a tree or a stone. He respects that on the path of life's journey the future is more than time, more than space; he knows that he will find his reality in those dreams that he creates and hatches. The aware combining of time, space, and self-energy permits a person to create from dreams the next step-of-choice on the pathway of present context.

Can the message of Zorba and Ulysses "Action is its own reward" be applied to the mass population? Or does it apply only to mythical heroes, or iconoclastic jousters? Some people believe such characters contribute nothing to the spin of life; others believe that without such models no human rhythm or progress would be possible. Productive action is the rose in

69

history's bouquet, the peaceful rhythm of harmony and balance is its fragrance, and awareness is its sunshine.

Living is a risky business. Embrace it! Ask it to dance! Share in harmony with it! Use your personality to balance life's situations, actively create opportunities and value. Take a number! Or set your own rhythm! Create a life! Let your personal choice of character be as refreshing as a cool rain on hot skin. When Awareness is, good choices flourish. Sizzle in your personal and inter-personal exchanges. Ride your dreams; don't chase them, and don't be chased by them.

Far too many people walk off the edge of life while staring back into the past. There are among us those who play the bad vibes game of all pain, no gain. They deal in disappointment, confusion, anxiety, false problems, seeking to make non-sense of sense (and vice versa) and neurosis of harmony. To create the pathway to the high mountain meadows of relating and sharing a beginning rhythm is: Chin up, eyes forward, move with enthusiasm and awareness. "To your marks! Set! Los!" Now, choose your pace! Flow! Listen! Harmony comes with Sharing (creating value). Balance comes with Relating (creating opportunity). Feel the wind and the rain in your hair. Dance with the Pyramids of Eenie, Meenie, Miney, and Moe. Step to the tune of creative Humor, Productive Activity, Patience, Respect, and Awareness.

**Writer's note:** In between the last word above (awareness) and this note, I took a 6000 miles, full-circle road-trip from Idaho, to Colorado, to Texas, to Georgia, to visit daughters, a granddaughter, relatives, friends, and business colleagues. These next paragraphs were drafted during that tour. I, "plucking the grass to know where sits the wind," set a rhythm which felt lifting beneath my worn and "woven wings." I used my favorite low-stress, grab-bag style of writing. But why am I telling you? You already know--if you've come this far--that's how I always present my pebbles along the pathway of our common journey. Shall we take the next step to the next pebble?

The title "The Loudest Hound" relates to how we seem to follow the gaudiest fad, the shrillest sermon, or the silliest fashion. Beware of the "madding crowd's ignoble strife." Don't put your dreams in a bubble, or cringe at the darting shadows of gossip and rumor. Sing in your own key. Don't let the opinion of others be your decision. Be aware, think, balance and formulate your own lifestyle and character. Listen to advice and to the voice of experience, but judge for yourself. Read the writers from the past and present to better select and shape a life's direction that leads to the blooming of your own creative spirit.

Too often we relegate ourselves to a life of passively staring at an open door hoping that a special someone will one day, one moment, step through it into our lives. Being a spectator of life is rich in unmet expectations, frustrations, and disappointments... moment after moment, after idle moment.

Avoid telling self and others not to experience the juices of active, creative living. Rather than telling others, "Don't put your hand in the fire!": Tell them, "It will hurt you." Let them decide and grow from the inside-out. No matter which way an "aware" person decides at a choice point--they grow,.. for they learn to decide, to experience consequences, to evaluate feedback, to move forward on their personal pathway of dreaming and productive activity. Living is not <u>rules</u>, it is choices. Rules are recommended choices based upon past results. When the standard rules fail, when the results of conduct and behavior become unacceptable, only the collective personal ability to make aware social and ecological choices will shape chaos into balance and harmony. Give self, others, and Nature something of value--accept and recognize (respect) contextual potential for social cooperation and ecological dignity--do not shackle the future with inflexible rules of temporary security from the past. Don't practice bad habits and poor form, whatever the game or pursuit.

Rhythm is change, not monotony. To stay in stump-dead involvements out of fear or for lazy convenience, to stay in a

71

despised job solely for security, or at a bad movie for the popcorn is, a reliable source assures me, a death march. My source holds twenty-seven "purple hearts" from the Crusades of the Emotions for disastrous choices in coupling... and for staying above and beyond the call of stupidity.

Like the old card player said, "You can't make a Royal Straight Flush out of deuces... or silk purses out of sow's ears, no matter how you strain or shuffle." Is your life being held prisoner in a burlap bag of trivial "busyness"? Who is setting rhythm? Who has drool on his whimper? Who has extra starch in her wimple? Why? Who cares? They are such a lovely couple, dancing the "Puke-on-your-shoe-tops" hop. Who's leading, who's following? Who's mentor, who's minion? Does it matter? Is living-well an "act of Nature," or is it created through aware choices? Helen Keller told us, "No pessimist ever discovered the secrets of the stars or sailed to an unchartered land or opened a new heaven to the human spirit." Yes, it matters, definitely. Who's setting your rhythm?

To "set your own rhythm" is an active expression of your awareness of: self in all aspects, your mood (your attitude), who you are and who you want to be in a given situation, a display of your values in a context... whether when alone or in a crowd, with others or with Nature. To "set your own rhythm" is to create your desired self-expression in aware concert with your context to maximize the social cooperation with others and your ecological union with Nature.

Mood is a reflection of yourself, your rhythm, spices, ingredients, your values, your context. Good mood is a balance and harmony between your physical, mental, emotional, and spiritual aspects of self as expressed through your social and ecological awareness with others and Nature.

Pay your social and ecological debts, large or small, as you create your living path, and you will have no need to look back in regret. To pick up litter is to paint a picture; to not throw it down is to dance with Nature, harmoniously. When you walk a path with a heart (social) and dignity (ecological) the best is always in the making. Do each thing in its own turn and time. Do what needs to be done, go where you need to go, accomplish and fail as you must... all in their own time and with awareness. Be young when it is time, listen when it counts, be wise when it is wisdom's turn, at whatever age or moment as awareness suggests. Then no debts will be held against the fulfillment you seek in living. Respect, humor, patience, and productive activity are the bridge, guardrails, and guidelines which lead to the joy of knowing self, and which place you on a living path of balances and harmony with others and Nature. Awareness is the center-line, the Force that moves you along your path toward the Summit of Good Hope.

How many people do you personally know who are actively seeking to create their next step in living? Who among your circle are not passively waiting for "something" to find them. And while they hope the "something" will be kind and gentle, they fear it will be "beer-breath, pms" bad.

Of the mass of people today who have "music" playing constantly in their ears, how many, do you suppose, are creating a personal and social rhythm which is not morally exhausted? Our "media" say, "Let both young and old be wired with this distracting sound-bath." The lesson for creating balance and harmony in-being seems to have become lost for them. To avoid the "heavy lifting" of setting their own rhythm some take the "exit" onto Fear's narrow detour--they rush-after the newest sound-track, or the oldest doxy. They want the "music" to do the job. They hope for rhythm and cooperation and dignity, too often they find only chaos and disappointment. This "doodah" deception is the "farm system" for many of our current politicians, it seems.

Don't be swept along in the tumbling tumbleweeds of the angry, embittered, or the narrow, naive thoughts and opinions of others. Look at the topics and ideas, each in the full context of your self-awareness, as they swirl in the marketplace like so many flies. (Hi, Mr. Nietzsche). Give them "Q & A" consideration, and if they enhance your social and ecological interest and productive activity then set your feet along these thoughts, awarely pace yourself, see where you arrive, and question and debate what you discover. Do not rush to the bait, or be blindly seduced by a melody of bias and prejudice... under whatever tent or rubric.

If you choose, awarely and deliberately, against an offered idea (e.g., the Nietzsche mix of God, death, and social motive) then heed the "Stop" sign before drifting in the rhapsodic eddy-currents of plodding idle-mindedness. To create the "good" life and to set your own rhythm is a life-long proposition that requires <u>all</u> of your time, space, <u>and</u> energy. It's the "Mother" of all dances. That it is better to be "fully lazy, than to be a lazy fool" is a swizzle stick philosophy not worth the stir. Awareness is informed action; lazy doesn't live there, it's not invited there, it's not welcomed there.

Set your own rhythm! Separate the flame from the smoke, the light from the heat. Avoid the trivial enthusiasms of the mindless mob; put serious distance between your pace and their frenzy. Laziness "speaks an infinite deal of nothing." Awareness teaches and creates more in a moment of silence than laziness forges in a life-time of babble.

Create your opportunities and values, provide your own motive, sight in clear awareness your life's purpose and direction. Otherwise the burden of daily disappointment will witness your passive tears as justice turns so readily away from you. The winds of a frantic, distressed society do not blow fairly. (<u>Stop</u> me! God bless conflict, risk, and choice.)

It takes self-trust and courage to say No! to peers, to friends, to others, to the madding crowd. Each moment that I don't trust myself enough to be in control of: my choices, my dance with life, my creative pace in context, and my death, is a moment I dedicate to fear. Saying No! is a key to personal pace-setting, and awareness is the lantern in the darkness at the crossroads of choice. Don't, in idle negligence, plant the seeds of Woe, when you wish to harvest the fruits of Joy.

All change, whatever its size or valence, is a <u>start</u> of a new involvement in the adventure in living. Ending an old relationship is not what we most fear; it is the starting of a new moment without a shield against loneliness that is most distressing. The flow of living is one of joining and separating, of birth and death, of hello and goodbye. Too often we look in the wrong direction for the solutions to our fears. Is it the distress of separation from the familiar, or is it the distress of joining with the strange that stabs us most painfully? Solutions of hope are impossible to create when a person embraces an attitude of despair. Against Despair's Goliath what David dwells in each of us? Give up the dark closets, the cross-dressing, the screaming of <u>mea culpas</u>: trot-out your Sense of Humor. Choose to "think funny," and failure loses its fearsome dimensions; choose to "set your own rhythm," and the success of "solution-creation" will champion any field or challenge. Let your Spirit dance, let your Spirit laugh... your pyramid is counting on it.

What does rhythm setting tell us about the Self-ological tides, the flow and ebb in living? What has a human history rich in thoughtful searching and theory building provided us about the fruits of our joy, the cinders of our woe? What can we trace confidently on our "canvas of Knowledge" about the hills and valleys of the human psyche? If we hold the rhythm setting model in mind when stress claws at the door, we know that we have choices. We can say either, "Not by the hair of my chinny-chin-chin am I going to let you in," or "Hello, darlin'. Do you want my butt in a sack or in a satchel?"

The dance of self, others, and Nature creates a contextual "psychic sweat" that runs: glad or sad, sweet or bitter, pretty or ugly, warm or cold, fragrant or fetid, and opp (other polar possibilities). Both joy, as nurtured by awareness, humor, productive activity, patience, and respect, and woe, as nurtured by fear, neurosis, selfishness, greed, and loneliness, are the offsprings of self (personal) and others (interpersonal) choices and rhythms. Ecological joy and woe--well, we are struggling with fear and pollution here. As the human head-count increases, the ecological body-count increases. To look at Mother Nature's problems is to find <u>us</u>--we're <u>it</u>. When looking at the curious art of relationship, rhythm setting and aware choices are marvelous pivots upon which to tie your understanding.

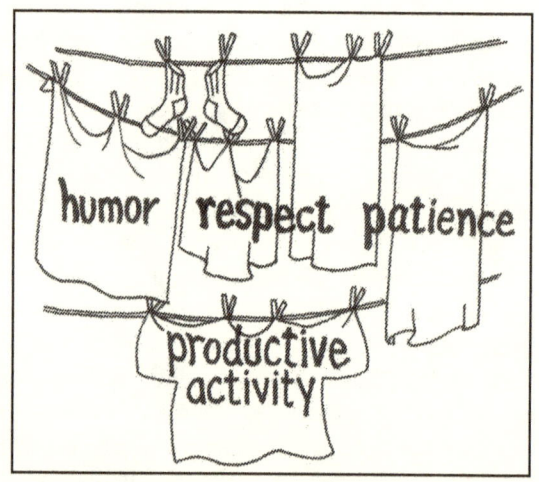

Your personal, interpersonal, and "internatural" actions, reactions, and interactions are the juice, the "sweat" in rhythm setting, harmony, balance, joy, or woe. The person who masters these strokes of engaging can awarely untie the knots, stir the wash, and hang-out the laundry to dry with humor, respect, patience, and productive activity.

All the other data is only so much neurotic soot and confusion. Spend no time on gossip, what-you-aren't-doing, choices-you-aren't making, or intellectual maze-mucking. Put not one ounce of living into either ignoring or attending to these backroad bandits of ignorance and deception. Problems are normal events in the classrooms of living--and problems always dwell in the past. They have had their moment... how else would we know them? Aware choices for change and rhythm setting have to do with the present today and the future todays. "Now" is when it's Show Time.

Balance in living cannot occur if you honor excessively any time-zone (past, present, future) over the others. We humans have memory <u>and</u> potential, and the sliding fulcrum of our present contains both our memories (past) and our potential (future). The aware person who sets a personal rhythm of social cooperation and ecological grace sits astride this flowing balance point, and happily says, "Scat!" to all other positions and styles.

What do you suppose would be a person's sense of <u>progress</u> whose total focus were the past; the sense of <u>purpose</u> of the person whose total focus were the present; the sense of <u>direction</u> of the person whose total focus were the future? Is such imbalance and absence of harmony really possible short of insanity? Is there even the slightest probability that a "normal" person can absolutely zero-out time zones of living? Can a person live completely in the "Here and Now" without any reference to the past, or glance to the future? "No," the fruit of many of my past dates, is my response. "No" is a handy reply to have in your arsenal; as are: "Whatever.", "Say what?", "<u>No</u> mas!", and "Katie, bar the door!"

In my experiences I have found that many occupations and activities have created "high-probability," recurring answers when a person wants a high-likelihood-of-being-correct response in a problem situation. Such replies can indeed be handy, at times usefully humorous.

Some examples are: In field artillery--"Drop five-zero and fire for effect!" In electronics--"One-half wavelength!" In football--"Drop back and punt!" In shooting a gun--"Correct for windage!" In psychology--"Have empathy!" In computer science--"Garbage in, garbage out!" In truck driving--"Double clutch it!" In picking a personality--"Go with the Brunette!" In placing a bet at the horse track--"Go with the three year old bay gelding!" At the dog track--"Go with the dog which most often has gotten to the first turn, first!" In mood-relationship improvement--"Set your own rhythm!" Do you know of others? Would "Don't force it, get a bigger hammer!" apply here? In what area? Living in general? As mere humorous commentary? Whoa! More sayings are pushing at the seams of my memory. "Can I <u>stop</u> ME?"

Ernest Lawrence Rossi, Ph.D. in "The 20 Minute Break" (p. 15-16) said, "Births, deaths, physical energy... mood... vary with the time of the year. Our mental capacities, emotional state, blood chemistry, muscle strength, eye-hand coordination... resistance to disease vary in predictable rhythms throughout each day." The idea of circadian (daily), ultradian (90-120 minutes), and infradian (monthly, seasonal) rhythms are known to be normal parts of the human living cycle. I have "zero-rythm" when it comes to remembering such classes and categories. How's your recall with such stuff?

How about the mood cycles we've experienced, or been told about? The Bio-rhythms are said to swing through a 23 days physical cycle, a 28 days emotional cycle, and a 33 days intellectual cycle. And as a wag once added: This doesn't include clio-rhythms... which are named for the circus clown who rides a 36" blue and white bi-<u>cycle</u> on a highwire. Pressure fronts are said to act on our glands and circulatory system, with the manic person being viewed as adrenal (diastolic), and the depressive person being viewed as serotonal (systolic). I'm glad I reviewed that, in case there are "pop" quizzes later in the day.

And how about the effect of light upon the thymus gland-- cabin fever is no "sing-along" for those who endure the extended gray days of a northern winter. Loud, long screaming at the icy night-sky does not count as a "sing-along"... even when done in a group.

We certainly are not separate from the world we occupy. How much does the natural environment affect our feelings? How much does the social environment ring our chimes? How do low pressure fronts impact you? Me? I get hungry, sleepy and slow-minded... seek shallow hibernation. Hmmm, I'm like that alot. I think I feel an attack right n....

The physically based rhythms, such as hunger, sexual arousal (Ultradian), sleeping and waking patterns (Circadian), and menstrual/hormonal peaks and valleys (Infradian) combine in expressed personalized mood swings, eating binges, winter blues (aka cabin fever), and the spring-time romantics of "running along the valleys, skipping along the hills."

Do these physical rhythms explain why so many people act like mindless toothpicks, in-a-table-top dispenser... waiting to be picked-up, used... then discarded by forces over which they have no say, choice, or control? Are the themes that turn-on your body, the same themes that turn-on your mind? Do you even know what themes, forces, pressures and seasons turn you on... mentally, physically, spiritually, emotionally, ecologically, or socially? Is the Force pulling you, pushing you, or crushing you?

Are we humans totally victims of a rhythmic context over which we have no say or directive awareness? Are we all simple captives of our physical cycles, or do such thing as awareness, music, smells, motive, or memories, for example, have a voice in deciding at which floor in the Mood Building of our existence the elevator of our rhythm will stop and present us? I have always thought of Nature as being neutral. Unlike humans, Nature has no moral wickedness, no sin: original, mortal, or venial. Nature can be seen as pleasant or nasty, lovely or harsh, delightful or deadly... depending on the time of year and a person's distance from the eruption, quake, or eye(s). Like someone said, "What doesn't kill you makes you strong. "Who do you suppose said that: Was it, A) Art Schopenhauer, B) Fred Nietzsche, C) Al Newman, D) Clark Kent, E) Madonna, F) a mime? The quiz was my doing. Mother Nature doesn't give grades; she doesn't care who sits, who thinks, who says. She just dances.

"Pop" psychology tells us, "Own your feelings!" This seems to say that we should make a choice now, because we didn't or couldn't make a choice somewhere in the past. It makes more sense to me to learn how to set my own rhythm and to take creative control of my feelings than to "own" them. Then, by personal choice, not by some expert's directive, I do "own" my moods and feeling, up-front... before, I hate them, before I sink into them like a cold stone sinks into a scum-pond.

Maintaining the mood to make creative choices is not easy. It is not for the lazy-minded, or the unaware, immature coward. Our lifelong habit and practice has been, largely, to look <u>outside</u> ourselves for the impetus to mood. We prefer to look to people, events, Nature, luck, and destiny (objects of blame), while ignoring the roles that awareness and self play in the mature pursuit of happiness. Nowhere in history can I find where joy has been the companion of the irresponsible, faint-of-heart person. James Norman Hall posed, "The thing that numbs the heart is this: /That men cannot devise/ Some scheme of life to banish fear/ That lurks in most men's eyes."

Why, do you suppose, we so readily turn over the control of mood, opinion, and thought to relatives, friends, questionable allies, and political leaders, or strangers? Could it be that we believe <u>blame</u> is the spice of the perfect recipe for the perfect life? "The Devil made me do it!" (Hi, Flip Wilson!) is the hub phrase of many world-class responsibility-dodgers.

When a person leaves the burden of his well-being to the world around him, he will find little playing time in the game of joy. It is the person who sets her own rhythm by creating opportunity and value who discovers that a high level of personal well-being is a constant. To blame is to be unaware and immature. Balance and harmony are fully absent in the Game of Blame; they're not even on the bench, or in the building.

The person in an interaction who brings all the creative energy, opportunity, and value to that exchange will become dominant... once the distractions, such as "immature" sexual intercourse jade. Thrills are too often followed by boredom; but creative rhythm setting, whether when alone, or with others, or with Nature, through humor, respect, patience, and the productive activities of aware learning, teaching, or doing, brings a fresh blush of beauty to life's cheeks every moment. Ralph Waldo Emerson told us, "Never lose an opportunity of seeing anything that is beautiful, for beauty is God's handwriting." And Loise Pinkerton Fritz said, "Birds He gave wings/ To soar to the sky;/ Man He gave thoughts/ To attain heaven's heights." Nice

80

stuff, huh? Have you seen any eagle soaring lately in your piece of sky?

Remember that to "set your own rhythm" is not merely another way to say: "Do your own thing!" Rhythm setting is actively creating and choosing the mood and attitude which you share in relating with self, others, and Nature. To "do your own thing" has its sole focus in spatial behavior. This saying was born in the 1960s in negative rebellion to perceived social limits and lies. It is not socially cooperative, it is an attempt to hold one's unaware breath until death or distinction agree to dance. Doing your own thing has an external behavioral-base of expression. Setting your own rhythm has an internal attitudinal base of feelings, values, and motive issues. There is a huge difference between <u>feeling</u> angry, and <u>doing</u> angry. To <u>do</u> angry usually infringes on the rights of others, while to <u>feel</u> angry does not. Road rage is to <u>do</u> angry. To drive America's highways without expressing rage is to <u>feel</u> angry, however calmly.

A basic assumption-flaw in prescribing "do your own thing" as a personal "social-creed" is that all <u>doers</u> will have respect for others, as part of the doing. The immature person has no such internalized respect for others. Therefore, a wide spread practice of, "thing doing" without awareness of social cooperation and respect for ecological grace leads to chaos. If chaos is your <u>thing</u>,.. please, don't <u>do</u> it near me. To set your own rhythm is to be aware of self, others, and Nature and to live in balance and harmony... using your time, space, energy, and choices to create opportunity and value.

A budding optimism is capable of bending flexibly in either the harsh winds of adversity, or in the joys of creative relationship. Optimism is a sign of maturity in the offing. Optimism casts its own shade, as well as its own light. The person who, in avoiding risk and challenge, seeks to hide in the nook of gossip or the cranny of rumor is a pessimist. The person who freely roams the field of creative living, from its blunt aggravations to its soothing pleasures, and seeks to savor the full challenge of both events is blessed with optimism. This person

81

truly "has a life" and is the envy of every pessimistic fool.  Fool?  Why a fool?  Pessimism, which spirals downward, can only get more painful.  Who but fools, and masochists, seek pain as pleasure?

Elegance is not found in the harsh, the callus, the selfish, or the abrupt.  Seek the gentle, the subtle, the smooth, the social in self and others, the grace in Nature and you will create a pathway of balanced vision, harmonious elegance, and ascending optimism.  How much margin does pessimism have for creating opportunity and value, relating and sharing?

Have you noticed how the "music" stops when someone in the group is <u>upset</u>?  What is the foundation of "upset:" optimism or pessimism?  Have you ever danced with "upset?"  How was it?  Some people believe that emotional upsets are based upon fear, failure, and a low sense of self-worth.  It is, indeed, rare to find social or personal theory that relates emotional-upset with success.  Do any come to mind?  If so, what formula for defining "success" was used?

The immature person does not seek to create an atmosphere of sharing, but solicits rather sympathy and uses blame freely.  "If you loved me, you'd feel sorry for me when I'm upset" is a too familiar line of muddied communications.  My silent response to a "by-choice" upset response is:  "If you choose upset--fine.  Enjoy it!  Don't demand my attention, participation, or sympathy.  My choice is:  indifference... just as being upset is your choice.  My choice fits me better."  Setting your own rhythm can be either negative or positive, indifferent or passionate.  Rhythm setting is not a frequent choice, however, for those who dislike change, maturity, responsibility; this is not a favorite path for the faint-hearted person who does not seek to grow, discover, and create Self fully in all its aspects.

Are you aware?  Some of the time?  None of the time?  How often are you rude, kind, humorous, sarcastic (the lowest form of ridicule, some believe)?  Do you over eat, then diet; smoke, then work-out; zig, then zag?  How often do you talk in active debate... with yourself?  Argue to a point of rage,.. or laugh with yourself? Awareness is the "Big Stir." Not as big, <u>maybe</u>, as the Universe, but big.

How dim or how bright is your awareness... of what events, thoughts, behaviors? How many times a day do you flush a toilet? How many squares of toilet paper do you use a day? How often do you drink alcohol, then drive? Has your cell-phone started leaving track-marks on your ear? How's your public nose-picking behavior? Still trying to give up the absent-minded habit of picking your pants out of your ass? How's it going? Are you the person you want to be... at work? with others socially? when alone? Are you a calm, creative companion called by many "friend," or are you a gushing volcano of anxiety and broken glass?

Some people make living a funeral march... others make it a parade. The events are the same, but the rhythm each person chooses to set his foot to is the difference... it is <u>all</u> the difference. We really do have a personal choice here. So choose awarely whatever works <u>socially</u> and <u>ecologically</u> for you. If you want a sad and heavy pace... sport that. Don't let others set your rhythm for you. Speaking of actual funerals, you can <u>do</u> respectful and polite behavior,.. but you don't <u>have to be</u> sobbingly sad. Unless, of course, that's your choice. Be <u>aware</u> of who's in charge and whose choice your rhythm is. Let the Big Stir of Awareness turn your context at a pace, tempo and rhythm, that sets your mood to dancing, your motivation to soaring, your creativity to laying-block.

The same weight that pushes your mood down, can, likewise, elevate you. How? Simply reach inside and change your location on the pulley-rope--living is ups and downs, pluses and minuses, gains and losses. It depends upon the rhythm you set, upon which end of the rope you choose to spend your time. Even the eagle comes down: to check-out a pyramid, pay taxes, rest a wing, sip an espresso, to attend a funeral.

What do you suppose the song, "Merrily, merrily, merrily, merrily... life is but a dream" means? Is it a reminder to set your own "positive" rhythm? Could it be saying that living is not etched in granite, soft clay, or even in mud? What is a person to think? Is living a flux of changes and choices in which we aware humans can create merriment in both our gains and losses? Can we, each of us, being in charge of our choices in a context design our mood, determine our own course, create our own rhythms? Or is living an out-of-our-reach nightmare, a black box of unconscious ugly tweaks and urges? If living is a flow of personal choices and awareness in context, why do so many people spend so much time in haunted houses and dark alleys? Can anyone, upon hearing four "merrilies" in the same song line, resist tapping a positive-toe and humming a light-lilt?

"Why do so many rhythm setters hum?" is an old poser. The stock answer is: "Because they can't remember the words." In my experience, humming is a major "relax-ative" of mind-mood. Humming is often the private mask, the <u>maschera privato</u>, of the thinker. Some people learn to hum, not just with their mouths, but also with their mind, their emotions, their spirit. It's a self-thing. These harmony-jockeys know the art of a stretching karma, a loosening mantra, a yawning yoga. This is stress judo, black belt class. Is your world a swamp or a garden? Are you on a diet of <u>Kraut oder Unkraut</u>? Are you gobbling stress-berries or smile-berries?

When the call "Start your engines!" goes out, remember: Start your <u>own</u> engine... in whatever the conditions. No one else can do it for you. It's your pace, your race. What's your Learning Curve? Are you a crotch-responder or a creative thinker? Are you a grunting knuckle-dragger or an aware "rhythm-nik?"

Take the drama, the stress, the heat, the worry, the friction that exist in a challenge-situation and make it work <u>for</u> you. Make challenge a motive of lightness, not one of darkness. Control the questions, answers, and the press of concern you measure in a moment's context by creating harmony and balance, using humor, respect, patience, and productive activity as the equalizers. Respond with the full awareness that both you and your rhythm are vital components of the very context in which you reply,.. and that it's your choice, your charge, your challenge. Being a mature, responsible person is marvelous exercise--I need to do it, be it more.

Some people have such lightness of spirit, an ineffable wraithness of well-being, which allows my mood to freely mingle and glide in the soothing dance of affection for living which they create and joyously emit. Others are not so elevating: their clogged rhythm-choice does not soothe me, does not bring me to relax, nor does it invite me to dance and reflect in humorous harmony. Is being a pinch-faced neurotic a path of balance and harmony? Does friendship bud, blush, and bloom here? It was Irwin Sarason who said, "Good friends are good for your health." Extreme Stress and Neurosis are not good friends.

We all tend more toward being of light-spirit and step when the world around us is spring-like and in-sync. Context matters. Does this also help explain the "quiet desperation," and the rut-nesting behavior, that holds such appeal for some people? If we are told that living is not challenge but routine, not risk but safe for all who walk a certain path, how many of us will ask, "Where do I sign up?" Some of us, hold both our breath and our tongue lest we make the whisper of a mal-content and lose our place in the prison of our rut. A conspiracy of silence.

But ruts are not risk-free and steady... in fact, ruts are down-right fickle. All ruts have Space, a few are wired for Time, but none has Energy. People who rely on the reflected-appraisal of an "outer world" as their sole index of self-worth lose the creative rhythm-potential of the golden thread between external complexity and internal simplicity. For such people, their mood platform is at best wet-tissue thin. "How do I feel about that?" they ask of others on every issue. They refuse to be Captain of their own rut niche, much less of their own rhythm, or piece of sky. Their desperation can approach Huge and Loud.

While each of us is unique and has to experience living in our own personal, special way--each to his own pace, each to his own rhythm--we all walk the path of life in the same direction: The direction of self-knowledge, social cooperation, and

85

ecological grace.    Some create their living pathway with awareness, humor, respect, patience, and productive activity, with heart and dignity. These, we call good, happy. These, we call fortunate, lucky. These, we call friend (if we can).

In setting your rhythm it helps if you remember that on some days, at some moments, at some choice points it is harder to create the poetry.  These are times when you totally miss the flow.  The golf swing is a metaphor for living:  Eagle-soaring one moment, turd-bobbing the next.  It is of such lumpy glitches that we talk to ourselves when later we review our "good" vs "bad" outcomes.  The words used, the feelings sensed at these review points add importantly to the practice effect so necessary in creative living. **You do review your daily flow, don't you?** The use of an immediate review (e.g., The manner and mood in which you answered a distracting telephone call.... Did you like the way you helped created the exchange?) doubles your experience, increases your awareness, brings your rhythm-goals into focus, and prepares you for the exchanges yet to be created in the moments, hours, days and life-time ahead. You can count-on, whether requested or not, a torrent of external "grades," some useful, some useless.  We humans are a free-floating critical-breed.  Self-evaluation, based upon outcomes and future possibilities, as affected-by your created opportunities and value, are your most important motivators.

How do you lift the spirit of self and influence others?  How do you find a corner of your Pyramid of Personality to grasp? How do you secure a handhold on creating your pathway?  How do you manage change and choice?  You do these things by **setting your own rhythm**. You monitor, adjust, and fine tune the mood/attitude, motive, and purpose over which you have control--your own. Others will give you (social at times, selfish at times) continuous feedback by their responses--they will adjust, agree, debate, decline, or follow your lead as they so decide. Accept nothing less--of others or of self. This is the way our tune and tone are created; it is an interactive input and feedback process of use and mis-use,.. and awareness is the filter, in both directions. Egad, in today's "sheeple-rush" for distraction and <u>altered</u>-awareness what might be "slouching toward Bethlehem to be born"? And borne.

Much of our daily stress comes from becoming entangled in the anxiety of others. We borrow it, we imitate it, we get caught-up in it. Avoiding the mire of other people's neurotic thoughts and behaviors is an achy-breaky aerobic-event. Supposedly, even our pets sprinkle our context with stress kinks and gravel.

For some people generating large doses of anxiety is a major daily motive for them. So be it! Leave it to them. Often these class-act neurotic will confide that they want to dump anxiety's burden, shed the addiction, and move far from the sting of its fangs. <u>But</u>... but, they add, they need a little help... from you. Do you smell the slight-of-whim? Here comes the part where you can get sucked in, slick and quick... <u>if</u>... if you  allow them to gain control over your filtering awareness-system and let them set your rhythm. Some anxiety-sharers are smoother than a spider with a flute.

To be able to recognize early in the dance that you are <u>not</u> in a creative, harmonious relating-environment is a trace clue of some existing wisdom and awareness in you. The gravity of hormones and sexual passion has a historic reputation for drawing zillions of our foolish, awareless fannies down the narrow hallway into the Vacuum of Horniness. Whenever I feel the cross-draft of alluring charm, whether it's of tornado force or a subtle breeze, my reaction is to check all the aspects of self for balance... and to ensure that I'm setting my own rhythm. Self-

87

sensibility tweaking is not paranoia pampering. When close-dancing with an "anxiety-virus" carrier, it's an act of pure survival. When I get keenly horny my awareness is the first thing that I tend to pull out of the game and sit on the bench. Age is no guarantee against foolishness. Only active, in-the-game awareness can serve that dessert.

Even well-lived persons can be found sinking to quick new lows (of his briefs or her undies) with rampaging hormone surges. When foolishness asks you to dance, don't flirt, don't blush, don't lead, don't follow. I suggest that you lean across the table, look "badnews" in the eyes, and kiss the situation goodbye. Don't look back, don't double pucker, and don't wink. Don't permit parting to snag a doubt, or temporary thrills to ambush your awareness. Parting, in the right circumstances, can ensure a stress-rout, a rush of pure ecstasy. Retreat is, at times, the wisest offense, the most aware defense. Honoring distress with your presence will not cause a miracle of "changing misery to joy." Here's an essay question for all you Road-ragers and Abuse-addicts: Does stress-absence or stress-overload register more often on your monitor, and why? You can check your answers with Bill Clinton and Mike Tyson, or Linda Tripp and Ken Starr. Please, answer in exactly 25 words.

It is said to be written on a wall in the Temple of Wisdom: "To try to unravel individual human problems in living is as useless as trying to pick the fleas from an Arab's camel." Human toil is vast and it demands flexible acceptance and recognition of its complexity. The human experiment cannot be solved by seeking to view it either through the eye of a tiny needle, or from a space platform. Balance and harmony are best thought of as being: neither too hot, nor too cold, neither too near, nor too far, neither too independent, nor too dependent, neither too extreme, nor too limited, neither too nor, nor too neither. Like the old Monk said," Strike a deal for moderation in all things, even in moderation."

Devotion to subatomic details and enormous kinks gives birth to retching anxiety and an obsessive, smothering style of interacting. The person who seeks to become involved-in and to hold control-over everything,.. knows little of and understands nothing about creating joy. To attempt to make living perfect is a vain act of self-serving destruction.

We hear talk of people marching to different drummers as they stride through life. Henry Thoreau drew interest to this idea, but said nothing about who is playing the drum, or how the beat is determined. How is your beat determined, each moment? Have you thought about it? Who is your drummer--Buddy Rich? Gene Krupa? Ringo Starr? The Four Horsemen of Rape and Run? Mother Teresa? Mr. Money? Dr. Who? Self? The Celeb of the Week?

"To live is to be borne upon the currents of a wind," it is poetically offered. A person cannot control the wind,.. but the more you understand the factors of context (forces and attitudes as they affect you) of living the better you are able to utilize the self to create opportunity and value, balance and harmony.

Man learned early in his existence on earth how to end a life. Cain, I believe, co-authored a landmark paper on the subject. Since way, way B.C. many (some clowns, some serious students) have worked to perfect this snuffing-skill. Others have, at the same time, tried to master the maintenance of life... even seeking to improve it. We humans are quite a stretch, aren't we?

Historically we humans have worshipped at two altars: that of death and that of life. Humans, in balance, seem more skilled at ending life, than in improving living. The success in this latter effort has been marbled and mixed. The vote is still out in heated debate on whether we humans have improved living one whit past a 5000-year-old detour into convenience shopping. And as to our clinically creating life, the blinds are still tightly drawn before our eyes. The angels laugh at our simple efforts to gain a year on eternity, and at our empty critique of the chess game between God and Satan. Vanity we're rapidly closing-on, but Wisdom appears to be <u>way</u> out of our league. Who wants to give up the chase? May I see a show of backs?

Awareness, knowledge, and understanding are good companions for the person who seeks to live more effectively,.. more fully creating self in all of its aspects along a living pathway with a heart and with dignity. To create opportunity and value within the influences of humor, respect, patience, and productive activity permits the progressive moment to remove the fear beneath desiring an eternally dependent existence. The pathway of living is not a thing, it is an experience. Joy and distress never dance together. You cannot choose both in the same moment.

The person who is aware of his context, thoughts and behaviors, the in-control non-psychotic, the person who holds a winning hand in the game of creating his social and ecological reality, can determine what mood he wants to express and what rhythm to step-to in any and all situations. Each person can, 1) create a living path, 2) set rhythm, and 3) select motive. We can each tune-in these three channels with one turn of our awareness dial. Awareness can be magical, and it's as pretty as free-will. It too requires daily self-practice, self-sweat, and self-stretching. In the ever-changing arena of Context it is truly "not over 'til it's over."

Living gets better as you get older,.. believe it or not. If (here's the pinch and the rub of the hive) you have started working at self-awareness, context discovery, rhythm setting, and the use of humor, patience, respect, and productive activity in your creative birthing of opportunity and value... as soon as now, if not well before, then Better and Older will dance together. You knew there had to be a stinger, along with the honey, didn't you? Bees are like that, and so is living.

If, as Henry Thoreau decided, "The masses live in quiet desperation" (or something close to this idea) does this mean that living is a totally desperate event... and that most people go from tick to tock only to exist, passive and unthinking, never seeking to turn away from the rutted course of desperation, never seeking to create a more active tree-lined avenue of living? Are we all desperate in living, perhaps, with a courageous few choosing to live in active desperation? Still desperate (In a desperate world, can it be otherwise?), but active rather than quiet. Doesn't viewing active desperation as the high point in living smack too loudly of pessimism? Is it old-coot flapdoodle and the prank of a child's dream to believe that together (Egad, stingers are everywhere) we can create a garden that buds, blushes, and blooms with more joy than despair? Have you tried it... lately? Ever? With a twist, or neat? Productive activity can replace distress with joy, dissonance with harmony, desperation with hope. I think Henry was lonely.

When a person sincerely smiles at the gripping challenge of the "low" moments in living that person is "far from the madding crowd's ignoble strife." That person has a firm grasp of the drumsticks that rap the beat to which she marches (Hi ho, Mr. Thoreau!). That person's self-spirit sets the rhythm to which she marches. I'm interested in meeting that person. Anyone can dance to "good times," it's those who can also dance to "bad times" whom I seek as models.

Anyone can start a race. Anyone can quit the race, when the course gets difficult and the trail long. These are things easily done, choices readily made. Pacing throughout the course makes starting a race a rational act,.. not empty boasting... and finishing serves as a seed for future confidence. Pacing and finishing are the heat and the light of the Torches of Living Experience that we each have the chance to pass to the generation of tomorrow. The challenges, long-of-fang, foul-of-breath, pound heavily against our way of life. Anyone for a little pacing? A little awareness? A little togetherness?

Anyone can start a race,.. ah, but to finish. To finish is opportunity created by pacing (awareness of self) and by the motive of being inside the effort. Smiles are born here.

Do you believe that the main theme of living is lost on most people? Do you believe that people are basically reactive in living, primarily responding (in quiet desperation?) to external stimuli, or to personal appetites? Is the purpose of our

91

educational-efforts to elevate personal awareness, or to train the masses (us) in accepted, habitual response-patterns? Does human existence better fit "soaring and creating," or "tweedling and cloning the dees and the dums?" What's your personal choice and what's your "druthers" for others?

Is passive reactivity the Adam's apple of why, at times, people do not cast a personal shadow onto their path of life? It is the variations and subtle shadows in living, certainly, that give dimension to the canvas of our journey. As we glance back along our memory track,.. some glances reveal no shadows, no dimension, no moment of ever having been. How do <u>you</u> define those of us who leave <u>no</u> "footprints in the sands of time"? How do we number, in your lean and view? How deep an imprint does the average Yahoo leave?

Without moments linked to other moments, living strikes a pose of "never more" (As Poe's Raven told us). How can such lack of dimension and linkage be the fate of so many of us? Perhaps, it is that, many of us approach living from the angle of rejection,.. not from the angle of respect (acceptance and recognition).

Perhaps those of us who "plod" along in the back of the crowd have been nurtured mentally, emotionally, spiritually, ecologically, and socially by coaches and contexts with no linkage to the times and events that we must "react" to in our present and our future. Did we have creative, progressive social models upon whom we imprinted,.. or do we carry a standard of living that no longer fits? Do the lessons of our primary teachers have even the slimmest trace of carry-over into the times of our lives? Awarely review your self-messages and decide if all your junk-mail has been dumped. To spend your time-space-energy in determining how many Yahoos will fit on the top of a bar-stool is not productively active, nor is it philosophically profound. Oh, and don't make a down-payment on the lie that "cream sinks to the bottom."

No matter how many lies I find attractive, I try not to dance with them... and I try to limit (to zero) the self-lies. I try to recognize the crooked little rascals for what they are: lies are game breakers. Failure to note other people's lies is naive; the failure to recognize your own lies traps you in the looking glass, and places the dreaded Jabberwock's foot firmly on your sophomoric throat.

When I am lie-free (for a day) I can see context more clearly and view with respect myself, my rank, and my century. When I am lie-free, I am self-aware. When I am lie-free I am like the old warrior who said, "I am the shadow-maker. I am one who paints the moments of life and gives them dimension. I last."

I've been told (by an espresso mainliner) that old songs last because they capture a <u>moment</u> in feeling. The secret to staying young at heart is in knowing that "moments in living" can and do happen at any time, at any age. While reactive people become weary and grow old in mid-plod, the active-creative person is too busy living to flag, to give up pace, heart, or dignity. To the risk-takers, the challenge-dancers, all decades of aging are potentially rich treasure-troves of self-worth and joy. Only cowards are snide. Only cowards lie. I really don't like being a coward. It's not a game I like to play, and the rhythm is lumpy and lacks "bebop." Oh, remember: Lies occur about the past-- it's exaggeration that fogs the future. When you spend your time in the past, you sit-out at the dance. Yesterday never dances. Yesterday only sits.

A reactive person cannot bring a <u>moment</u> to

the active person, but many <u>moments</u> can be given the other way around. We have spent billions of dollars on more billions of student-hours training students to abandon their childhood curiosity and to become fully "reactive" adults. The signs at our school portals too often read: "Check your uniqueness, curiosity, and creative potential before entering." As a result, the United States has depth and ample reserve in its "spectator" pool. The business world and the advertizing spin-artists of the marketplace have made huge profits from this situation of communal passivity. Reactive people tend to be social parasites who do not do well when left alone with the demon of their boredom. Productively active people, conversely, who awarely create their own living moments, find that living has meaning and bebop-joy... whether alone or in crowds. The "TV remote control" is not high on their list of "The Human Race's Most Important Inventions."

There exist numerous and amazingly quick ways to sink your rhythm to a one-note drone. Try any combination of lack-of-awareness in events involving self, others, and Nature and you'll be an immediate quest-lecturer in "Screw-up 101"--the catacombs of character catatonia. Likewise, there are a gang of ways to wind your rhythm so tight and frantic that the migraine mainspring pops. For example, try getting caught-up in other people's anxiety,.. or better,.. getting caught-up in your own anxiety. Nature, as far as I've seen, doesn't waste time on anxiety in any form... probably doesn't know even how to spell migraine.

If we know what we're doing, why do we choose not to use the attitudes and behaviors that help elevate our interactions with others and with Nature? Most of us are, at best, selective and time-limited in our use of additive social and ecological talents and skills. Why not, for example, catch self, others, and Nature "being good"? Why not increase the likelihood of daily success? Why be pleasant to a passer-by, and "slime" a friend, spouse, or otherwise-relative? Why not be socially and ecologically enhancing and aware in all interactions? Are we interested only in "short-term" profits from strangers, with the more permanent people and places in our living-routine on notice to "beware or be damned?" Why don't we create a personal path with heart and dignity? Are we too "phobiaphobic" to treat others with heart, Nature with dignity? Have you noticed that most of my Q's are quizzical statements, not questions of inquiry? They seek action, not words.

It seems that we only choose to be aware of permanent-social creating when a situation begins to die, to rot, to explode, to corrode, or to get terminal rash-of-the-crotch. A wiser choice is to awarely, actively set a rhythm which enhances positive exchanges in all cases--short and long term. If you want living (a moment-to-moment proposition with life-long endurance) to be additive and joyous keep the following simple doing-point in mind: Positives add, negatives subtract. Knowing the difference can be trickier than zipping or unzipping a garment,.. "so, please, be kind."

As is widely known, a person can be an SOB, or a Bitch, if you're "guy-thing, girl-thing" sensitive, without any help. I can do this negative lean. You can do this, too. So why ladle this negatory, non-creative portion of your personality onto others? And why permit others to burden you with similar abuse? Some choose to dance with life, others prefer to "bitch-it-out." Pissing in a cut is neither remedial, nor creative. Recognizing the difference between "being pissed-off and being pissed-on" becomes a lifestyle priority for those people who like being enraged. Could this be a high-tech topic for a Ph.D. thesis? Are we nearing a break-through in understanding human nature?--Fat what?

It has been said, in poetry, prose, and graffiti, that life itself is a game, a play with people as actors who strut, posture, stumble, prance, and fret. Some actually dance. Is acting what we do? Nothing else, more, or less? Are those of us who appear to be more in tune, harmony, sync,.. at peace... are they simply better actors? Do their pace, rhythm, and awareness permit them to more readily create opportunity (relate) and value (share) with others and Nature? If this is so, then let us study their dance

95

well. If living is no more than creative acting, let us act the good-act. Let us heed the drummer's beat, let us be aware of our cues, let us set a personal rhythm of social cooperation and ecological dignity. The "Great Pretender" does not have to be a melancholy, self-interested liar. Let's not be victims of daily bad acting, and reap only terrible reviews from future generations once the final curtain rustles down on our brief moment.

Door keys and social models serve similar functions. A given key opens a given (lock) door; a given type of model can set your foot on a given path of behavior and attitude. Certain keys open doors to happy family rooms; others, doors to dungeons. Certain models show the way to joyous living; others, will give you chronic personality gas. Select your models with awareness. Observe the social feedback and outcomes available to them, and evaluate the social and ecological impact they create. Become a model for others, and evaluate your <u>own</u> social and ecological influence. Choose styles awarely.

If, for example, you want a full, socially active life style, do not adopt as your sole model a reclusive monk. You may not like dancing to such a rhythm. All people are not meant to be monks, nor are all people meant to be cheerleaders. Know your self, and set your own rhythm in joyful ecological union and social cooperation. Remember: "Some like to bebop, some like to blame, some like to sits."

Some things are done despite the contradiction against their being done. An old Latin saying, that has this slant, goes: "<u>Credo quia absurdum</u>..." "I believe <u>because</u> it is absurd." Usually we "pass" on the absurd option, but should we <u>always</u>? Dreams, in example, are said, by some, to be <u>un</u>real. Do I accept that idea? Do you accept it? Who is the Rhythm Master on your pathway of living? How can dreams not be real? By the way, what <u>is</u> your definition of reality? Anyone for the impossible?

Rhythm and the law. I recently read of an old carry-over St. Louis law that cites: "You cannot drink beer from a <u>bucket</u> while <u>sitting</u> on a roadside curb." To my knowledge the law says nothing about drinking from a Dixie cup, or a hub cap, for that matter. "They're at it again! The lousy @*#=,#*:! are pickin' flaws in our laws!" some unhappy, negatory types might chafe as they escalate their blood pressure to the aneurysm lift-off point. My reaction is: Who drinks beer from a bucket while sitting anyway? I always stand-up to do that. My point is: Don't spend energy fretting at silly gnats. Such actions put chains on your choices, drains on your energy, and your rhythm sinks to a monotone. Mantras don't have to be one-note hums of monotony. You decide which fights on the play-ground you want to become embroiled in.

Lilly Tomlin (comedienne) is credited with having said, "No matter how cynical you are, it isn't enough." This seems to be a think-about-it line. I wonder if Ms. Tomlin knows a friend of mine, who years ago offered: "You can never be cynical enough to stay up with the assholes among us. They are endlessly inventive. They stay up late plotting how to ambush us in the market place each day. It's the assholes who have all those office building lights on 'til all hours in every city across the country--in case you wondered--plotting!" This fellow also has strong opinions about many conspiracy issues. Rumor, from good sources, has it that this youngster, at age 79 years, is charged with having assaulted a hot dog vendor at a baseball park. Who sets a cynic's rhythm?--Ah, who the hell cares? It was my friend's Uncle "Red" who gave us the line: "There are so many assholes in the world, I wonder if I'm not one of them." It must be in the genes, huh?

97

*Nalli*

# Rhythm Thresholds And Awareness Transition

In applying an approach, method, or attitude to a social problem, such as one might use the "tough love" approach with problem teenagers, you will find yourself mixing personal rhythm setting with social philosophy/theory offered by others. It helps to remember that you don't use a method to "get it to work" at "any cost" to your personal rhythm and sanity. You are better served to select a method because it is what <u>you</u>, not what others, have determined and chosen, after aware consideration, as the best rhythm for you in the given situation and circumstances.

Avoid being sucked-up by techniques, fads, or fashions that do not fit or enhance who and what you are. All rhythms do not work for all people. All styles and sizes do not fit everyone, nor does one style or size fit all. Ever spend a day dancing in Alice's or Dorothy's slippers? "Ouch!" is the only lesson, for me. You are seeking to set your own rhythm, in dealing with your teenager (in my tough-love example), based upon external information and advice. No matter what the hype, the outcome message and measure is in <u>you</u>--the doer, not in the youngster. Success buds, blushes, and blooms in motivated, productively active dancing. Each context is special, and a "bigger hammer" is not always the best method for getting the finest fit.

The question is: Did you set the rhythm that best suits your personality, context, and choice? Do not seek to gain control-over and to force others to change in the direction you want. Are you an autocrat, a tyrant... must all roads lead to your outcome desires? Or are you a model for "set your own rhythm" within a contextual awareness of ecological union and social cooperation? "Quick-fix" often results in "quick-disappointment."

Do not get caught saying or thinking in despair, "Hell, it didn't work!" If you set the rhythm that you wanted, then it <u>did</u> work. How others are influenced by the rhythm you set is <u>their</u>

99

choice. When setting rhythm, hang tough. Read the external and internal contextual feedback, read your feelings, your purpose, and trim as is needed, by your choice, but keep on keeping-on, awarely. You choose: ride the bull, or coo with the dove. Whoever made-up the "strokes and folks" adage had certainly sucked an egg or two.

Ideally, in my opinion, in the architecture of a building... thresholds from one area, from one function of living, to another should be employed. These transition-thresholds serve as introductions to the function into which one is entering. Such as from eating, to socializing/relating, to relaxing, to studying, to toilet and bathing, to sleeping, to playing, to etc. This is not accomplished by using repetitious rectangular doors. To have the means and the money to use internal foyers, drapes, cloisters, alcoves, nooks, tunnels, windows, archways, and various patterns of stairs, ramps, spirals and sunken floors... in a dwelling-place is a pretty dream of purpose and plan. To have transition-thresholds in creating self... ah, such marvelous images leap to mind.

Transition-cuing could be created within the abstractions of self by having a threshold into an idea, a mood, a relating moment. In some cases and moments we do this, and we do it rather well. The crossing of a specific threshold gives us clues of what to expect, how to act, what we know and do not know, what we desire, how keen our focus, what we can learn, what we can teach, and what we can do. These thresholds are also known as AWARENESS triggers. Let me give a "for example"--most of us have some experience with "sex-stuff"... the crowded planet tells me so... and some of us understand the value of "foreplay." I ask you: what is "foreplay," if not transition? What is the taking of a Viagra-booster, with an hours lead-time no-less, by some of us older coots, if not transition? The list can be quite lengthy... and laps-over into and onto every social, ecological, and personal activity and assorted-stuff. Transition is important to rhythm. The more aware a person the more subtle the thresholds he/she can react-to, create, and sense in a relationship context-moment.

In communicating, my canteen runneth over with "for examples," we often use cues: Cues to topic, cues to shifts in subject matter, and cues in the form of definitions for lighting the way from point to point. Without threshold-cues to guide us our conversations and words run endlessly into the hard walls of emptiness, confusion, or misunderstanding. Hit any walls lately? Cocktail party "Chitty-boom" is one massive maze of walls, the hits come often,.. no transition. "Chitty-boom" is mostly noise, vocal-cord exercise with little behind it, nothing in front of it... but "The Wall." You may have guessed: I am not a "Chitty-boom" fan. I see "Chitty-boom" as verbal pollution, loneliness in words. RSVP? You bet--if it's "Chitty-boom" hour. I ain't comin'!

Sex, as practiced in intercourse, is an event for which almost everyone, excluding brutes and acorns, develops a threshold. We cross the threshold, some claim we do it far too readily, and invite a partner to enter that dimension with us... with specific ideas and intentions. When we recognize the sensation: Horny,.. we like to have others join us--potluck, usually, posthaste, usually. Color me naive: is sexual vigor gaining the upper-hand over social virtue as a priority in our wisdom years? Some priority, some wisdom, some pyramid.

Thresholds, awareness triggers, are the cues to activities, thoughts, and creations. Sex is an early and compelling event-urge for us. It is a skinny-gauge train we eagerly, often awarelessly, ride to the platform of our desire's fulfillment. But far too often, for far too many of us, we camp out for a life-time on the single platform of sexual-interacting to the harsh neglect of the other marvelous aspects of self in relating and sharing with others and Nature. For some Sex is the only voice they hear in the darkness. The cue threshold to sexual intercourse is usually a single-note, one-dimensional howl at the moon... not

101

real subtle. Sexual-urges and Fear can be found close-dancing rather often, more than we like to accept.

The threshold of a body of water is the surface of that water. If you dive, fall, or are thrown through that threshold, what does it tell you about what you might want to consider doing next? If the water is shallow, you may be meeting-up with a new,.. much harder threshold abruptly. If the water is deep and salty you may discover a new, exciting threshold in the form of a hungry shark. All thresholds lead into possibilities, endless circles of choices and context. Living with awareness is never boring. If every breath is a threshold, a different threshold... what do you do with that? How many circles can you identify in the daily swirl of your living currents? How many thresholds do you deal-with, or sense? How many "swing thoughts" can you master? How many dances can you endure? How large a pyramid can a person build?

Set your rhythm by defining and perceiving your personal thresholds,.. those that you will cross, those that you will not cross. In living, thresholds are choice points. To live well a simple awareness serves one far better than a superior ability to blame. Be aware of extremes, and of those dreaded bites that are too big to swallow.

No relating (creating of opportunity), or sharing (creating of value), or productive activity (aware learning, teaching, doing) occur in many of our buildings (our bureaucratic fortresses) because the thresholds--structural and interpersonal--are blurred, or non-existent. Most offices are boxes for containing: 1st) furniture, and then 2nd) bodies. Rarely do offices give a cozy embrace to ideas and personal interactions. There are exceptions, but most structures provide warehousing without animation. No wonder bureaucrats drink so much coffee. Caffeine does help to alter one's reality... as many drugs do.

Telephones are yet another peeve of mine... in the universe of thresholds. I dislike telephones because there are only narrow, skinny-boned thresholds to cross. Too quickly can you plunge-in upon others, or you get plunged-in upon. Telephone talk, for the most part, is a hollow exchange of words without thresholds of social cooperation or ecological union. I don't like that game. If you agree: Press One! Just a moment, let me put you on Hold. And how about radio and television? Click! "Hey, 'lax, mon. It be muffalala time! Altered boredom be our specialty." Quaff another electronic-cocktail, Bubba, Bubbette.

Our rituals and traditions are stepping-stones across the thresholds of the spirit. Marriage and family are excellent examples of this. We have socialized thresholds in our concept of "Rights of Passage." This demonstrates the importance we humans have historically placed upon the social value of thresholds. Today we ignore largely the moment-to-moment social thresholds, long honored as necessary to good order, in the interest of Blur.

Living is a continuous crossing of thresholds,.. the next moment doesn't exist yet, and that moment is a threshold to be crossed, to be created. How we cross it, how we create it is our choice. The more aware a person is the more threshold opportunities and value they may create. The more thresholds a person manages and experiences the more socially and ecologically marvelous the potential. I have a thought--Let's <u>do</u> some golf-thresholds together sometime, shall we? Golf is a continuous series of thresholds; so is creative living. Anyone interested in some threshold-respect? Cooperative social adventure and unified ecological dignity in living equals awareness that soars with the eagle, thresholds of prettiest bud, blush, and bloom. Context is critical to rhythm. To be the only flower in a garden of weeds is a deadly struggle of deep lonely.

*Nalli*

## Rhythm Exercises and Practices

"When you can't scratch,.. the itch seems all the more intense" is a saying I've just made-up in the interest of silliness and sanity. A small snag can gaff your rhythm when you turn your pace-control over to the wrong-result models. To finish this book, to get-on with running up my lantern, to help create a social and ecological forum with heart and dignity is becoming a major itch. Any suggestions about help in scratching? We all know: 1) Select your rhythm models based upon their outcomes, 2) Words and wannabe-stuff should never exceed productive activity on your selection criteria for forum models, and 3) Avoid the closet nail-biters and butt-pickers when choice points and thresholds beckon, "Come!" Ah, my Kingdom for a final period. Where is my Eagle? My Queendom for a soothing scratch.

As you experience living you see effective and not-so effective people--you see sad and glad, open and glum. But do you see destiny, luck, or choice at work in our communities,.. is a combination of these factors apace? Does the army of "therapists" know anything worth paying for? Or are we dancing with mountebanks, mavens, and charlatans? Where are the "coaches in living" who can assist losers to become winners, and winners to become champions? Where are the itch-scratchers, FCOL?

We need coaches in living and models of social cooperation and ecological dignity who can influence people to set their own rhythm and make aware choices in the direction of patience, humor, respect, and productive activity. As individuals we need to use every model, hint, and experience to create our path with a positive pace and rhythm.

Aldous Huxley, I believe it was, said, "It is not what happens to you that is experience, it is what you do with what happens to you that is experience." Huxley seemed to be a fan of active living rather than passive existing. To improve our personal

105

condition in living we must embrace the fact that we, each in our own fashion, are <u>always</u> creating the moment.

Who is giving you your "game plan," your "pep talk," your "curds and whey"? Are there any coaches or friends in your locker-room? As an individual, a couple, a family, a team, a community does anyone influence you in experiencing how to make choices, change direction and pace, read feedback, and set your own rhythm? Do you ever practice various mood and attitude expressions? Do you habitually pass an empty collection plate?

What do the current acknowledged coaches, the teachers in our social and ecological stream, bring to us? We practice reading, writing, mathematics, some physical education, some play-mating (usually free-run... but "No hitting!")…. We can practice ballet, swimming, various sports, as are available, and assorted scouting programs. And our churches round it out with praying. Are there any coaches-teachers who demonstrate and guide us in consolidating <u>all</u> the known aspects of self into creating enriched character; Personality Building? Where are the pyramid builders of our age? Met any wisdom, lately?

Are there any practice times for smiling, listening, anger, lightness, pouting, joking, laughing, crying, teasing, respecting, thinking, planning, sharing ideas, being rude, being social or ecological, etc? Living in a society and relating and sharing effectively is to <u>act</u> a part, a role. We call this role: Personality. Each of us learn our social and ecological role and we create its traits of character as a results of our degree of context-awareness from our birth (some believe from our conception) forward, moment-by-moment. Parents and family are, indeed, our first teachers; home, our first classroom.

Why do we not have classes and practice rehearsal-times... throughout life... that meet the questions: How do I <u>want</u> to <u>feel</u>... in various contextual moments? Who is in charge of my mood, my attitude, my personality? How assertive toward that wanted feeling, mood, attitude, and personality is my <u>best</u> effort? How do I get to "know self" and how do I create a "living path with a heart and dignity"?  May I have this dance?  May I introduce you to my pryramid?  Would you be interested in soaring with the eagles?

Being socially cooperative and ecologically unified have many do's and many don'ts.  As primates we, by our nature, are able to do many of the don'ts, but where can we learn to do more of the do's?  Can the don'ts be shaped into do's?  What is the difference between social cooperation and mass control? Control does not give you answers, control limits your questions, while cooperation encourages questions (a natural human trait). Cooperation is the best context for creating effective answers, moment-by-moment.    Humans can be responsive to broad (national) top-down control, but small-scale cooperative-contexts (communities) are better for insuring positive social outcomes in living.  Fear has been and is the primary tool used by the control-tyrants of history.  Cooperation thrives on inquiry and freedom. Can the human race continue, if it <u>does not</u> destroy Nature?  Can it continue, if it <u>does</u>?

Living cannot be done with words alone.  Why talk, if words don't carry the message?  When I was a young boy growing up in a small town in West Virginia I worked daily on learning how to "cuss," to hold forth a tough image, and how to use "big" words to hold forth an educated image.  As I've grown older, I can see that neither cursing, nor long words (sesquipedalianism) are rhythm enhancers for me.  I try to curb both the "spit" and the "polish" by using clear statements in place of obscure ones. As you have witnessed in reading these pages, I still have miles to go.  Four-lettered words still seduce me at times despite my failure to understand a single "damn" reason for using most of them.  Eagles don't need four-lettered words, FCOL.  Maybe if I were to increase the <u>Tia chi</u> in my diet and make more "lazy circles in the sky."

To have a rich <u>passive</u> vocabulary is a treasure of great worth.  It provides an anchor of confidence in taming the word-storm that assails us every moment from the "gutter to the summit" of our market place.    Rhythm-setting enjoys

107

confidence. Word-awareness is also a useful companion when tilting with SATs and GREs and other tests of the like. To define words in a personal style join them with social and ecological events and actions. Build your vocabulary as you build your pyramid.

I've found that putting fun-words in place of slum-words, and seeking solid clarity of thought over vague labelling is more who I am and what I want to be. Instead of saying, under (or over) my breath, to a rude passing-stranger, "You jerk-ass son-of-a-bitch (or bitch, as dictated by gender)," I try to smile to myself and respect the hurried life-style and bad rhythm that results in rudeness. I'm not yet a master of this art, but I'm trying. I would prefer to say (under or over) "It's another doo-dah day, Mike." As for big words used to impress but not to illuminate, I prefer to hold hands with Ennie, Meenie, Miney, and Moe than with the Four Horsemen of the Apocalypse (I looked up this spelling). Some big words are a perfect fit, most are as nothing. And like the saying: Ex Nihilo Nihil Fit tells us, "Out of nothing, nothing comes." Define your words with your productive activity. Set your rhythm with awareness.

How can a person use "visual imagery" to set their own rhythm? Why would you want to? Someone once said, "Exercise is preparation. The prepared person is rarely surprised." Sounds like something General George Patton may have framed. You can reduce your panic, your startle-reaction to uninvited events by mentally rehearsing a rhythm you prefer to create in imagined, but potentially actual, situations. Use visual imagery to prepare (a rhythm) for situations, good and bad, which may suddenly, without warning, leap into your world. For example, the death of a loved one, a loud noise, an automobile accident, winning the lottery, a fall in the mall, a bird dropping a load on your date's shoulder, meeting Ms./Mr. Marvelous, tripping down the escalator, etc. How do you want to behave and flow in certain unexpected situations? You can anticipate the random... think it over. Rhythm is within you. To practice, or not to practice is one of your daily choices. You do practice for the expected, don't you?  So why not give a moment to the unexpected--thoughts can travel at pretty impressive speeds.

When I was growing up, during the 1940s, there was a radio show called "Let's Pretend."  It was on the radio each Saturday morning (as I remember it) and the Nally kids (there were five of us then) would gather to join in the fun of the radio imagination exercises and magic.  There were times when I even pretended to be "Cream of Wheat," which was one of the Saturday show sponsors.  What did I know?  When it comes to pretending and imagination anything is possible... especially for a curious young child.  And as I've aged, I've tried never to lose that edge of adventure into the self.

Learn through practice... aware practice, not routine repetitions of "bad habits."  Learn by rehearsing, as an actor learns roles, the mood and rhythm you want to display and apply in given situations.  To live well takes effort, constant effort and energy... but it's damn well worth it. (Darn that cussing!)

How are you with a John Wayne or Gabby Hayes line, or a Scarlett O'Hara monologue to slow your internal wheels and calm the pace of events?  Can you apply a laid-back California surfer's hair-shaking attitude of casualness after wiping-out violently (purling) only to eagerly strike-out to catch another wave?  Is silence, coupled with active, alert eyes, part of your message-delivery system?  Marlon Brando is good at this film form.  Or do you just blindly do "etc" as you and events crash and form the context of the moment?  How's it working for you, whatever it is that you do?  Are you up to your choice speed, or are you in the "later-than-usual" crowd?

Call up your favorite preferred models from memory.  Use them and their quotes and styles to aid you in setting your rhythm.  This exercise teaches you to cross thresholds, prepared to create a sensitive, effective attitude and rhythm of your choice.  Don't be someone you aren't, don't be someone you don't want to be.  Don't be "Cream of Wheat" when you prefer being "Reddi Kilowatt," or Marlon Brando, or Mother Teresa, or Elmer Fudd, or You.

Morning wake-up is the "starting gun" for setting your own rhythm. If you slink out of bed with snake-slit eyes and a slumped, empty mood-of-despair wearing a hangover and hell-class bad breath it is easy to think: "Life is heavy! I'm depressed! I hate this!" My hope is that you will put some air under your mood. Meet this "moment of truth" by choosing and using the "up" key to "start your mooder" (I couldn't resist). You're at the "a.m." choice point, a new threshold--whatcha' gonna' do?

Set your rhythm first thing upon waking--don't let those sleep-breaking whiz-trip to the bathroom "grouch you up," nor the wee-hour crying of a newly arrived infant. Be glad your plumbing is working. Same with the baby, be it a request for clean diapers or more food. Be pleased. Thank your genes for what are indeed the most unbelievable of miracles. Why have a bad attitude about positive things? If there is no Heaven, no after-life, then just waking up is cause a-plenty for celebration, in my view. This is why, perhaps, we have such mysteries.

Our wake-up rhythm tends to stay with us as we engage our schedules, so why not get in charge of your mood and set the rhythm you like... early. If your choice is a pissed-off, I-walked-into-a-wall mood,.. fine,.. but please don't bring your pygmy social-awareness into my context formula... I really don't need it, thank you. I've got all the mood-pollution I need. Oh, checking and setting your rhythm periodically throughout the full course of a day is also helpful in keeping you out of the ditches, and away from head-on rage-crashes with others.

I'm more inclined to choose "UP" rather than "DOWN." I work better that way, and I find being "UP" more effective than being otherwise. Use a sign on the ceiling above your bed, if necessary, to remind you to set your rhythm and mood to a socially cooperative level... I'd appreciate it, in case we cross moods during the day. My bedroom sign (an imaginary one) says, "Don't think depressed, think crazy!" When I look at my morning-face I remind myself, "Think up!" It beats the splints out of being depressed all day. We're in a stress ambush of social mashed potatoes and de-spined personalities, as I see it, and we need all the hedge we can get. Try it, please!.. I can use the help. To "have an attitude" in current usage means: negative, does it not? I suggest that the positive opposite of that attitude state is called: Friend... and I'll take all I can get.

An old gardener once told me, "Son, go beyond the trestle, the trellis, and the gazebo." I think my grandfather was telling me to go beyond the usual, the routine, the trite... but with his heavy eastern European accent... I was never sure. But as far back as I can remember, I've enjoyed talking to the wind and whispering to a fallen leaf or a blooming flower. My joys are words and thoughts and behaviors that serve as reminders to good pace, to good rhythm, to good living, to self discovery. I enjoy a context that helps me maintain and create my rhythm of choice.

It may just be a quirk of my increasing years, but I find that I prefer grace to crude, poetry to porno. In parting company, I'm encouraged when people choose to say: "May the winds caress your flight," or "May the warm rains nourish your fields," or "May an angel kiss your dreams;" instead of "Sit on it!" or "Up yours!" or "Scumbag clone!" I think the old gardener's message was: Be creative, keep thinking beyond habit, reflex, and the routine rut. What you say, think, and do doesn't have to be dull, if you choose effort over ease, <u>Kraut</u> over <u>Unkraut</u>.

Have you heard the comment "Let's have fun!"? Does this have the same external origin as "Let's have lunch!"? "Fun" is not something you <u>do</u>, as I understand it. "Fun" is an attitude, a rhythm-set which a person can create each moment within a context. People can "do" lunch, "do" sex, "do" exercise, "do" etc., but we can't "do" fun. Why the look? Are you having trouble with this notion? Tell me about it.

As a young child playing in the sand box, for example, you created fun,... Until sand was thrown in your eyes. Ah,.. ouch! then "playing" became un-fun. The rhythm-set, the attitude was broken--for you. Anything can be fun, if you choose to have it be. Sand in the eyes, even. "It's fun, what I'm doing" is our

111

turned-inside-out way of giving external events credit (blame) for internal attitudes. Am I having fun, yet? You can bet your sweet grits I am. This book is nearly finished, and I'm liking that possibility. I can always tell when the rhythm I want is paling--I start cursing more intently. Oh,.. by the way, I think there is such a thing as "positive anger." How do you vote on that? Why? Played any bad golf lately? Does anger help?

Is it possible to "make" others comfortable, as in "feel better"? Who sets whose rhythm, in fact? When you find yourself assisting a person in dealing with illness, or aging, or life's aches and wrinkles, or death of a loved relative or friend is that person setting there own rhythm, if they become dependent upon you? Are you able to set your own rhythm with such responsibility for dependent others? My answer to both questions is: Yes, the choice is <u>always</u> personal. Dependency and responsibility are choices. Let your awareness of this "choice-right" influence you to create value and opportunity in every situation. Avoid burdening others with their choice of dependency, and avoid blaming them for yours. Sharing is a great way to get all parties and partners to "move off the nipple."

Whenever I do socially additive acts, small or large, such as recycling, not littering, picking up a nail from the street, saying hello and smiling at neighbors, talking to barking (fenced, lonely, and bored) dogs, permitting other cars the right of way or to merge into my lane of traffic, wishing silently hurrying strangers well on their journey... or in general creating spots of opportunity and value... I've been known to say: "I deserve good things to happen to me (occur in my context)." Quite often they have been known to do just that.

I'm pleased to report that I've discovered, when I'm fully grounded with my "inner" net of productive activity guided by respect, patience, and humor, that good things are <u>always</u> happening to me. My path of choice is rich with abundant challenges and my awareness is always eager to take yet another creative step into the moment's context. Ah, what good fortune I have the responsibility to share. Rule #1 in the manual "Positive

Personal Engineering for Making Living Happen" is: AWARENESS... and Rule #2 is: SET YOUR OWN RHYTHM.

A popular school of psychology teaches us that it's what we think about events that causes our feelings in response to that event. "Thoughts cause feelings," they say.... Which puts the event in the trigger position to stimulate thoughts which, in turn, create our feelings (about the event?). Or are our feelings related only to our thoughts? What does the school of notions say about that, I wonder? Are all events totally neutral? Well, in any case, the model used is a simple A-B-C design: A(Event)-B(thoughts)-C(Feelings).

This concept certainly is loaded with social learning overtones and influences,.. do you agree? The idea is far from new. In fact, some credit the slave Epictetus (circa 60-120 A.D.) with the framework's creation. He may also have been the initial philosopher to say: "Walls do not a prison make; nor chains, a slave." Epictetus was a huge fan of attitude's impact on our well-being... despite events, however negative.

How do you suppose a person can prevent undesired feelings from intruding in the course of her daily behavior and interactions? How does a person set the rhythm of choice when events surprise her? Are there events which may, or may not, occur in your context, your life-space, such as a mugging, a car accident, a burglary in your home, a sudden death in the family, a plane crisis (with you strapped in seat 13A), a crushing illness, a surprise birthday bash, a class reunion, a job loss, a divorce, a relocation to new digs, or even a sharp noise that you would like to be prepared for physically, mentally, emotionally, spiritually, and socially? I can assure you, there are many such events, that I, in my rhythm-personality make-up, want to have some idea of how I'll feel and behave should they occur.

My choice-mode for preparing an attitude, a thought-net is through pre-event practice. I believe that each of us can decide how we want to react, no matter what the event entering our context. We've been told, "You can never know how you'll react to pressure, stress, or crisis." I don't agree. Why bother to train (practice combat) soldiers, if it is useless; or rehearse for a stage play, or practice a sport's event, or an interview, examination, or speech, if it is so much foolishness? Despite our hustle-butt, haste-'til-you-waste lifestyles, we all have "sits and think" time. I use some of mine writing letters, some rehearsing, some bebopping, and some being mugged by addictions.

We get prepared by practicing and pre-selecting the attitude, feeling, and response of our choice. This is what training is all about, in any endeavor of living. This is what school is supposed to be--learning that can be translated into effective performance expressed through the aspects of self within a context. Heart and dignity, balance and harmony are not genetic windfalls lucked-upon by a few special souls.

To set your own rhythm is to get in front of the results of living, to get inside of creating opportunity and value in a context influenced by humor, respect, patience, and productive activity. Today our life-style and market-place motive of profits over people has gained control by being out-of-control. An interesting twist of extremes and why we need to choose moderation, quality over raw quantity. This is not "destiny" at work, this is human "choice-force" of active, awareless chaos in the blush.

Living is our most important game. It is the only game in which we must play all the moments we are alive. "Don't bother to prepare yourself. It's impossible to create a relationship in living of harmony and balance, and social and ecological rhythm," our negatory mavens tell us. "Shit happens! and you're stuck with it." Prevention doesn't sell as well as Cure in the world of the Clueless. Rehearsal, rhythm, and awareness are Prevention sorts of doing.

What fools we are if we permit the gossip of intense pessimists and the rumors of the defeatists to cast us into a "mood motel" of personality poverty. Rehearsing, practicing, and aware rhythm setting are necessary in doing any game well, and they are invaluable blocks in one's personal pyramid for influencing the context and outcomes in the game of living.

Rhythm setting, pre-and-post, provides you with choices to be dauntless in the face of present challenges, however short your lead-time. To be afraid of something, be it animal, vegetable, or mineral, does not have to render you stunned and dumb in its presence or occurrence. Let fear influence healthy, aware caution in your choice of dances with that particular partner or context, but don't let it <u>control</u> your life, or any part of it.

Rhythm setting is a masterful antidote for the "willies."

The rhythm you set in any situation is your personal choice. For example, I am to attend a funeral. I want to set a rhythm of caring and love, a rhythm of being confident and comfortable. I loved my friend in life, I will love my friend in death. I have come too far in living to any longer need to personalize the death of others. So I choose to celebrate my friend's death in joyful sorrow. Personal confidence does not deny sadness or tears, nor does it cause me to ignore the rhythms set by others. The rhythm I choose will be socially aware and respectful of what others choose to do and what they feel comfortable with.

I do not want external events (only a part of my context) to trigger thoughts and attitudes that I have reactively adopted without awareness or testing of worth. I want to be the trigger, the attitude, and the doer. I want to set my own rhythm and be responsible for the final shaping of the context in which I live. It takes practice.... Improvement is possible.... It is good.

Living is the most powerful and complete game you'll ever be a participant in. All games take energy and awareness to do them well. Awareness and preparation put fear on the run. You don't "get a life" ...you "create a life." And each of us is doing that at this moment... whether we're aware of doing it or not.

If you aren't going to take charge of your living context, who will? If you aren't going to go for the whole <u>tamale</u>, who will? May I see a show of hands of those interested in "setting your own rhythm." No timid souls need apply. All rhythm setting takes is time, space, and energy... and a dab of aware courage: Nothin' to it!

Now it's "pop quiz" time. Clear your desks, please. Question: Which personality would you rather be: 1) The small mouse that roars, 2) The young bird that can't fly, 3) The old dog that won't hunt, 4) All of the above, 5) None of the above, 6) An itch, or 7) A scratch-er? In Atlanta, Georgia a few southern-fried types claim the saying: "Some people scratch an itch, some people itch a scratch... and only God and Scarlett O'Hara can do both." Most Georgians deny any personal responsibility for such "crawdad bait" sayings. They "blame" backwoods education for their "red-neck" neighbors' belief-choices. I bet these same people have trouble deciding if "the poison is in the flagon with the dragon, or in the vessel with the pestle." Gosh, I enjoy Danny Kaye's pace and style. But enough. Time to close.

Let me end this with some quotes: "You cannot prevent the birds of sorrow from flying over your head, but you can prevent them from building nests in your hair." (Chinese,.. of course)

"The more I practice, the luckier I get." (Unknown source to me. Please help me, if you can.)

# P.S.

"You are in your own way. Please, stand aside." (Fortune cookie classic) Have you set a rhythm, or driven a mood lately? Yours, preferably. An appropriate reply to "I'm in a bad mood," a clue of some awareness, whether said by self or others, is: "And?"

May the gentle winds caress your flight and may the warm rains nourish your fields. Good health, good choices, and good journey until the next book. Now that we've come this far together, let's stay in touch. Like the song says, "My baby likes to bebop,.. and I like to bebop, too."

Hey, Pudge! Call me!

*Nalli*

# ABOUT THE AUTHOR

Mike earned a Ph.D. in psychology about 25 years ago; in living he is still earning his wings. He believes that it is time to shell the nut of awareness,... and to move into the forum of the new century with chin up, head high, and eyes on the challenges that would thwart us from reaching for the greatness of our human potential. Mike is a flexible poet with no set meter, who believes in the positive possibilities of social networking. He was born in 1938 in West Virginia and he now lives in Idaho. He is interested in joining motivated others in creating a forum of awareness and energy for the mutual joy of opportunity, sharing, heart and dignity. Mike's lantern is up, and turns slowly in the winds of change and choice. Mike is contact friendly – try him.